T

BAKING
ONE STEP AT A TIME

BAKING
ONE STEP AT A TIME

THE ULTIMATE STEP-BY-STEP COOKBOOK

MARIANNE MAGNIER-MORENO
PHOTOGRAPHY: FRÉDÉRIC LUCANO • STYLING: SONIA LUCANO

✳ ✳ ✳

hamlyn

TO JÉROME

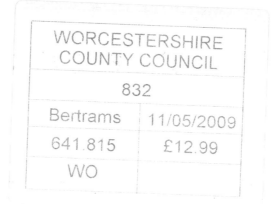
First published in France in 2007 under the title
La Pâtisserie, by Hachette Livre (Marabout)
Copyright © 2007 Hachette Livre (Marabout)

© Text Marianne Magnier-Moreno
Photography by Frédéric Lucano
Styling by Sonia Lucano

An Hachette UK Company
www.hachette.co.uk

First published in Great Britain in 2009 by
Hamlyn, a division of Octopus Publishing Group Ltd
2–4 Heron Quays, London E14 4JP
www.octopusbooks.co.uk

Copyright © English edition
Octopus Publishing Group Ltd 2009

ISBN 978-0-600-61953-6

A CIP catalogue record for this book is available from the
British Library

Printed and bound in Singapore

10 9 8 7 6 5 4 3 2 1

Measurements Metric and imperial measurements
have been given in all recipes. Use one set of
measurements only and not a mixture of both.
Standard level spoon measurements are used in
all recipes.
1 tablespoon = one 15 ml spoon
1 teaspoon = one 5 ml spoon

Nuts This book includes dishes made with nuts and
nut derivatives. It is advisable for those with known
allergic reactions to nuts and nut derivatives and
those who may be potentially vulnerable to these
allergies, such as pregnant and nursing mothers,
invalids, the elderly, babies and children, to avoid
dishes made with nuts and nut oils. It is also advisable
to check the labels of preprepared ingredients for
the possible inclusion of nut derivatives.

Eggs should be large unless otherwise stated. The
Department of Health advises that eggs should not
be consumed raw. This book contains dishes made
with raw or lightly cooked eggs. It is advisable for
more vulnerable people, such as pregnant and nursing
mothers, invalids, the elderly, babies and young
children, to avoid uncooked or lightly cooked dishes
made with eggs. Once prepared these dishes should
be kept refrigerated and used promptly.

Milk should be full fat unless otherwise stated.

Butter is unsalted unless otherwise stated.

Ovens should be preheated to the specific
temperature – if using a fan-assisted oven, follow
manufacturer's instructions for adjusting the time
and the temperature.

FOREWORD

I love baking but many times in the past it seemed that baking didn't like me…
I strived to produce well-risen, springy scones but they came out flat. I really tried to
produce gorgeously textured chocolate mousse: it was too dense, or too dry. In the
face of dozens of disappointments, made all the more frustrating because I
followed the recipe instructions scrupulously, something nevertheless kept a spark of
hope burning: in the midst of my flat scones, there was always one much higher than
the rest; among my failed chocolate mousses, one of them seemed to murmur to me
'You're on the right track'. The right track maybe, but which one? The mousse stayed
silent, the scone implacable. I felt as if I had met a brick wall.

In baking terms, this 'wall' is all the books, recipes, classes and workshops for both
professionals and amateurs. In a nutshell, the wall of the novice pastry-cook is a huge
ocean of advice and ideas, sometimes contradictory and often false, in which you
have to immerse yourself in order to discover the hidden secrets. I dived in.

By picking my way, from equipment to icings, I made it through the pastry-
cook's maze. It meant taking copious notes, comparing, absorbing and, above all,
experimenting ceaselessly. From these discoveries, some principles were established
and I never ignored the invaluable advice from top pâtissiers. I learned, for
example, the secret of chocolate mousse: the egg whites must be supple not firm if
you want to fold them easily into chocolate; the chocolate-eggs-butter mixture must
be warm and the egg whites must be at room temperature. Quite literally, I ran home
to try it out. I hovered near the fridge for the required amount of time and, a few
minutes before the specified time was up … I tasted chocolate mousse that was, at
last, a success! For my scones, it took an American cookbook to get me on the
right route: the dough must be thick and the scones must be small (3–4 cm/less than
2 in) and the oven very hot (at least 220°C (450°F), Gas Mark 7). Miraculously,
my scones came out of the oven tall and proud and – the ultimate test – crumbled
into two under the slight pressure of my thumbs.

The book in your hands today is the product of copious effort, both patient and
passionate. It has therefore for me a special worth, one that I hope you too will value
once you have tried the recipes. My wish is of course that the results will be the finest
baking in the French and English traditions but above all, that it gives you that multi-
tude of tiny details without which, in baking terms, there is no magic.

Marianne Magnier-Moreno

CONTENTS

1
CREAMS & CO.

2
SIMPLE CAKES

3
LAYERED CAKES

4
LITTLE CAKES

5
TARTS

APPENDICES

GLOSSARY • TABLE OF CONTENTS
RECIPE INDEX • GENERAL INDEX
ACKNOWLEDGEMENTS

CREAMS & CO.

CREAMS

Vanilla custard 01
Confectioner's cream 02
Butter cream 03
Almond cream 04
Lemon curd 05
Chocolate mousse 06
Chocolate ganache 07
Panna cotta 08

SAUCES & TOPPINGS

Caramel 09
Salty butter caramel sauce 10
Chocolate sauce 11
Red berry coulis 12
Red berry compôte 13
Chantilly cream 14
Plain icing 15
Chocolate icing 16

VANILLA CUSTARD

❧ **MAKES 400 ML (13 FL OZ)** • PREPARATION: 15 MINUTES • COOKING: 15 MINUTES ❧

300 ml (½ pint) milk
1 vanilla pod
3 egg yolks
60 g (2½ oz) sugar

IN ADVANCE:
Gently heat the milk in a saucepan with
the vanilla pod split open and the seeds
scraped out into the milk. Leave to infuse

(if possible for 10 minutes) then bring
to the boil. Remove and discard the
vanilla pod.

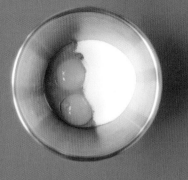

1 2
3 4

1	Put the egg yolks and sugar in a small bowl.	2	Beat them thoroughly until the mixture is lighter and has slightly thickened.	
3	Tip half the boiling milk in a thin steady stream onto the egg yolks, whisking all the time.	4	Transfer the mixture back into the milk pan over a medium heat. Allow to thicken, stirring constantly.	➤

☞ Make sure you scrape the base of the saucepan, especially at its edges, with a flexible spatula because that is where the temperature is highest and where the risk of coagulation of the egg yolks is greatest. The more the cream heats, the richer it will be, but there is the risk of it boiling and hence scrambling.

Watch the fine moussy trail that forms on the milk/egg mixture. When this mousse disappears, the custard is approaching 90°C (175°F), the temperature at which you must stop the cooking.

IS IT COOKED?	**COOLING**
Dip a wooden spoon in the custard then run your finger down the back of it: it should leave a clearly visible line. The custard is ready!	Strain the custard through a fine-mesh sieve over a bowl and leave to cool, stirring from time to time. Cover and refrigerate (for no longer than 24 hours).

CONFECTIONER'S CREAM

❧ MAKES 700 G (1 LB 8 OZ) • PREPARATION: 10 MINUTES • COOKING: 10 MINUTES ❧

500 ml (17 fl oz) milk
6 egg yolks
100 g (3½ oz) sugar
50 g (2 oz) self-raising flour

OPTIONAL FLAVOURINGS:
40 g (1½ oz) praline
3 small teaspoons coffee extract
or 125 g (4½ oz) chocolate, melted

1 2
3 4

1	Bring the milk to the boil in a saucepan. Meanwhile, whisk the egg yolks with the sugar until thick and creamy. Incorporate the flour.	2	Pour half the hot milk onto the eggs, whisking constantly. Return to the pan, still whisking (scrape the base of the pan to stop it sticking).
3	Continue to whisk and allow to boil for up to 2 minutes to achieve the required consistency: the more the cream boils, the thicker it will be.	4	Transfer the custard into a bowl and stir in your choice of flavouring. Cover with cling film, placing it directly on the surface, allow to cool completely then put in the fridge.

BUTTER CREAM

❧ **MAKES 300 G (10 OZ)** • **PREPARATION: 20 MINUTES** • **COOKING: 5 MINUTES** ❧

125 g (4 oz) butter
1 whole egg + 1 egg yolk
2 tablespoons water

100 g (3½ oz) sugar
½ teaspoon vanilla extract (or use half
vanilla extract and half coffee extract)

IN ADVANCE:
Soften the butter to a pomade then whisk it
for 2–3 seconds. Whisk together the egg and
the egg yolk in a bowl with a pouring lip.

1
4

2
5

3
6

1	Put the water then the sugar into a saucepan.	2	Cook to the 'ball' stage, then pour the sugar onto the eggs.	3	Beat with an electric whisk until the mixture is chilled and has trebled in volume.
4	Pour the mixture in a stream over the softened butter while continuing to beat.	5	Add the vanilla extract or vanilla and coffee extract and beat again.	6	Use immediately.

ALMOND CREAM

❧ MAKES 300 G (10 OZ) • PREPARATION: 15 MINUTES ❧

75 g (3 oz) butter, softened
75 g (3 oz) ground almonds
75 g (3 oz) icing sugar

1 egg
1 teaspoon cornflour
1 teaspoon rum

1 2
3 4

1	Use a wooden spoon to work the butter until completely smooth in a medium bowl.	2	Sift the ground almonds and icing sugar through a fine sieve over the butter.
3	Mix with the wooden spoon until the mixture resembles wet sand, with a few pieces of butter remaining. Add the egg and mix well.	4	When the cream is homogeneous, incorporate the cornflour and the rum. Cover with cling film and store in the fridge.

LEMON CURD

⟞ MAKES 300 G (10 OZ) • PREPARATION: 15 MINUTES • COOKING: 5–10 MINUTES ⟝

4 egg yolks, carefully separated to remove
all trace of whites
5 tablespoons lemon juice (1–2 lemons)

125 g (4 oz) sugar
rind of ½ lemon
65g (2½ oz) butter

STORAGE:
Once completely cold, the lemon curd can
be stored in a sealed jar. It will keep for
2 weeks in the fridge.

1 2
3 4

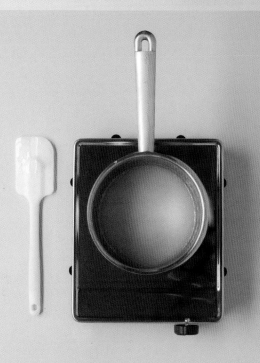

1	Beat the egg yolks in a small bowl then pour into a pan through a fine strainer.	2	Stir in the lemon juice and sugar. Put the pan over a medium heat. Stir with a flexible spatula for 5–10 minutes, scraping the sides of the pan.
3	Run your finger down the curd on the spatula: you should see a clear trace if it is cooked. The curd will continue to thicken as it cools.	4	Remove from the heat, then stir in the lemon rind and the butter, cut into cubes. Allow to cool in another bowl.

CHOCOLATE MOUSSE

➥ **MAKES 300 G (10 OZ)** • PREPARATION: 20 MINUTES • COOKING: 5 MINUTES • REFRIGERATION: 2 HOURS ↤

125 g (4 oz) plain dark chocolate (minimum 70% cocoa solids)
50 g (2 oz) butter

2 egg yolks
3 egg whites
20 g (scant 1 oz) caster sugar

IN ADVANCE:
Cut the chocolate and butter into small pieces. If the eggs are cold, plunge them into a bowl of hot water for a few minutes.

1	Put the chocolate in a small saucepan and allow to melt over a very low heat.	2	Add the butter and incorporate with a whisk. Remove from the heat.	3	Add the egg yolks, one at a time, whisking between each addition. Allow to cool.
4	Whisk the egg whites until they are supple, adding the sugar halfway through.	5	Fold in a quarter of the whites into the chocolate, then fold in the remaining whites until just incorporated.	6	Divide the chocolate mousse between individual ramekins. Refrigerate for at least 2 hours.

CHOCOLATE GANACHE

❧ **MAKES 100 G (3½ OZ)** • PREPARATION: 5 MINUTES • COOKING: 10 MINUTES ❧

50 g (2 oz) plain dark chocolate
(minimum 52% cocoa solids)
1 tablespoon single cream
50 ml (2 fl oz) milk

IN ADVANCE:
Break the chocolate into pieces.

1 2
3 4

1	Put the cream and the milk in a small saucepan and bring to the boil.	2	Remove from the heat and add the chocolate. Stir until it melts.
3	Return to a medium heat and cook for 2 minutes after it bubbles, stirring all the time with a flexible spatula.	4	Use immediately or pour into a small bowl and cover with cling film placed directly in contact with the ganache. Leave to cool in the fridge.

PANNA COTTA

➤ **SERVES 4** • PREPARATION: 15 MINUTES • COOKING: 7 MINUTES • REFRIGERATION: AT LEAST 2 HOURS ✦

2 leaves of gelatine (5 g/¼ oz)
1 vanilla pod
400 ml (14 fl oz) single cream
65 g (2½ oz) sugar

IN ADVANCE:
Soften the gelatine in cold water.

Break the vanilla pod and place in a pan with the cream.

1	Heat the cream with the vanilla in a small saucepan over a medium heat.	2	When the cream starts to steam, add the sugar and whisk to dissolve it.	3	Increase the heat. Once the cream simmers, remove the pan from the heat.
4	Leave for 1 minute, remove the vanilla pod and add the drained gelatine (squeezed first between your fingers).	5	Whisk the cream vigorously to ensure the gelatine is thoroughly incorporated.	6	Allow to cool for 5 minutes, whisking once or twice to prevent a skin forming. ➤

7	Carefully pour the cream into 4 ramekins or little pots, whisking frequently to ensure the vanilla seeds are evenly distributed. When the creams have cooled to room temperature, cover them with cling film and refrigerate for at least 2 hours.	**IS IT SET?**
		Remove one panna cotta from the fridge and gently shake it; the cream is set if it does not quiver when you shake the ramekin. You can turn it out or return it to the fridge until you are ready to serve.

| 8 | To turn out the panna cotta, fill a heat-resistant bowl with boiling water. Remove the cling film from the ramekins. Dip each one into the water (not quite to the top) and wait for 8–10 seconds before removing. Quickly invert onto a plate. Gently shake the dish until the panna cotta is released. | **NOTE**
※
If you use moulds that are less thick than ramekins, the heat of the water will warm them more quickly, so dip them for only 3–5 seconds before inverting onto plates. |

CARAMEL

❖ **MAKES 100 G (3½ OZ)** • PREPARATION: 5 MINUTES • COOKING: 5 MINUTES ❖

2 tablespoons water
100 g (3½ oz) sugar

EQUIPMENT:
Have a pastry brush handy to wet the sides of the saucepan with water: it helps to remove the sugar crystals.

TIP:
To clean the pan, fill it with water and bring to the boil. Whisk to remove the caramel then tip everything away.

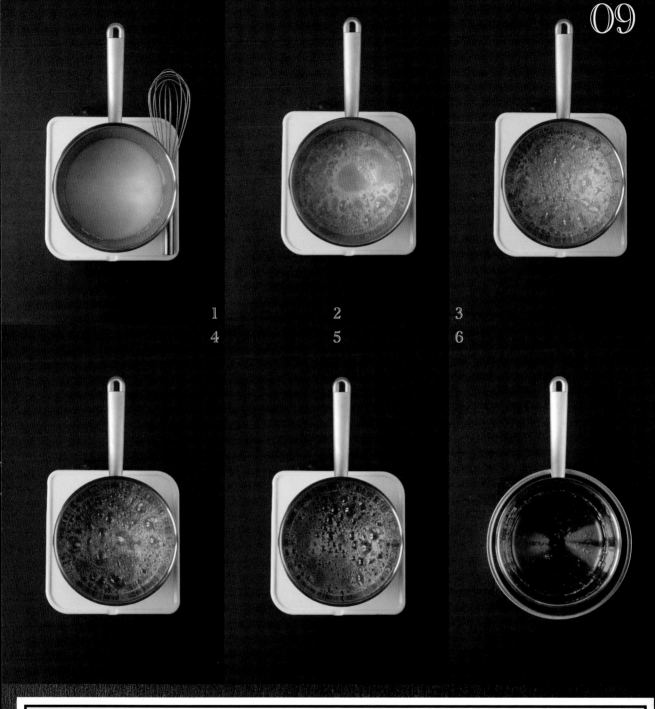

1	Put the water then the sugar into a small, heavy-based saucepan.	2	Place over a gentle heat and whisk until the sugar dissolves.	3	Bring to the boil while wetting the sides with the pastry brush dipped in water.
4	As soon as it reaches boiling point, stop stirring immediately and allow the caramel to colour.	5	Plunge the base of the pan for a few seconds into cold water to stop the caramel cooking.	6	Use as quickly as possible; the caramel will harden as it cools, making it difficult to work with.

SALTY BUTTER CARAMEL SAUCE

❋ **MAKES 200 G (7 OZ)** • PREPARATION: 5 MINUTES • COOKING: 10 MINUTES ❋

15 g (½ oz) salted butter
100 ml (3½ fl oz) single cream
2 tablespoons water
100 g (3½ oz) sugar

IN ADVANCE:
Cut the butter into small pieces.

1	Pour the cream into a small saucepan and heat over a medium heat.	2	Put the water and the sugar into a second small, heavy-based, pan.	3	Whisk the sugar and water over a gentle heat until the sugar dissolves.
4	Bring to the boil. Stop stirring immediately and allow the caramel to colour to a rich mahogany.	5	Add all the hot cream. Mix with the whisk and leave over the heat for 2 minutes.	6	Remove from the heat and add the butter. Mix and allow to cool (the caramel will thicken on cooling).

CHOCOLATE SAUCE

❧ MAKES 300 G (10 OZ) • PREPARATION: 5 MINUTES • COOKING: 5 MINUTES ❧

100 g (3½ oz) plain dark chocolate
90 ml (3¼ fl oz) milk
100 ml (3½ fl oz) single or whipping cream

IN ADVANCE:
Break the chocolate into pieces.

1 2
3 4

1	Bring the milk and cream to the boil in a small saucepan.	2	Remove from the heat and add the chocolate.
3	Mix with a flexible spatula until the chocolate is completely melted.	4	Return to the heat. Remove as soon as it starts to simmer. Use quickly.

RED BERRY COULIS

❧ **MAKES 200 G (7 OZ)** • **DEFROSTING: 10 MINUTES** • **PREPARATION: 5 MINUTES** • **COOKING: 1 MINUTE** ❧

200 g (7 oz) frozen mixed red berries
50 g (2 oz) sugar
pinch of salt
½ teaspoon lemon juice

IN ADVANCE:
Put the frozen fruit in a heat-resistant bowl and place the bowl over a pan of boiling water. Cover the bowl with cling film and leave to defrost – this should take around 10 minutes, stirring after 5 minutes.

1 2
3 4

1	Sprinkle the sugar and salt over the defrosted fruit while still in the bain-marie and mix for about 1 minute to dissolve the sugar and salt.	2	Transfer everything into the bowl of a food processor fitted with a blade and mix for about 20 seconds until the mixture is blended evenly.
3	Rub through a fine sieve using a flexible spatula to crush the purée and extract all the juice.	4	Add the lemon juice. Mix well, cover and put in the fridge for at least 1 hour. This coulis will keep for 4 days in the fridge.

RED BERRY COMPÔTE

❧ **MAKES 250 G (8 OZ)** • **DEFROSTING: 10 MINUTES** • **PREPARATION: 10 MINUTES** • **COOKING: 5 MINUTES** ❧

230 g (7½ oz) frozen mixed red fruits
25 g (1 oz) sugar
½ teaspoon honey
2 teaspoons balsamic vinegar

IN ADVANCE:
Put the frozen fruit in a heat-resistant bowl and place the bowl over a pan of boiling water. Cover the bowl with cling film and

leave to defrost – this should take around 10 minutes, stirring after 5 minutes.

1 2
3 4

1	Drain the fruit, reserving the juice. Mix 40 ml (1½ fl oz) of the juice with the sugar, honey and vinegar in a pan. Place over a medium heat to dissolve the sugar, whisking occasionally.	2	Bring to the boil to thicken it. To check it is cooked, dip a small spoon into the pan and bring it out again; the syrup should coat the back of the spoon.
3	Leave to cool before adding the drained fruit. The syrup will thicken further on cooling.	4	Mix together. When the compôte is cold, cover with cling film and place in the fridge.

CHANTILLY CREAM

❖ MAKES 550 G (1 LB 2 OZ) • PREPARATION: 10 MINUTES ❖

50 g (2 oz) icing sugar
1 vanilla pod
500 ml (17 fl oz) crème fleurette, chilled
(or whipping cream, or use one-third
double cream to two-thirds milk)

IN ADVANCE:
Fill a bowl larger than your mixing bowl
with ice cubes and very cold water.

TIP:
To make a small quantity of Chantilly
cream, use a bowl with high sides and
dispense with the cold-water bain-marie.

1	Put the icing sugar in a medium bowl and add the vanilla seeds scraped from the pod.	2	Plunge the base of the bowl in the prepared frozen water and pour in the chilled cream.
3	Tilt the bowl to maximize the amount of air and whisk using an electric whisk on its highest setting.		**CHANTILLY IN A SIPHON** ※ Pour the cream, sugar and vanilla seeds into a cream siphon. Close and attach the gas capsule according to manufacturer's instructions. Shake vigorously.

PLAIN ICING

✤ MAKES 100 G (3½ OZ) • PREPARATION: 5 MINUTES ✤

½ egg white
100 g (3½ oz) icing sugar
1 teaspoon lemon juice

FOR A THICKER ICING:
Add up to 25 g (1 oz) extra icing sugar

STORAGE:
This keeps for several days in the fridge or for a month in the freezer in a sealed container. After refrigeration, rework the icing with a little icing sugar.

1	Put the egg white in a bowl and add the icing sugar.	2	Mix with a wooden spatula for 2 minutes until you have a white cream.
3	Add the lemon juice at the end and beat for 10 seconds.	4	Trickle the icing over your cake, spreading it with a palette knife. Allow a few minutes for the icing to set before serving.

CHOCOLATE ICING

❖ **MAKES 200 G (7 OZ)** • PREPARATION: 5 MINUTES • COOKING: 10 MINUTES ❖

100 g (3½ oz) plain dark chocolate
40 g (1½ oz) butter
75 g (3 oz) icing sugar
3 tablespoons water

IN ADVANCE:
Break the chocolate into pieces and cut up
the butter.

1 2
3 4

1	Put the chocolate in a small saucepan and melt over a very low heat (or in a bain-marie), stirring with a flexible spatula until smooth.	2	Keeping the pan over the heat, add the butter and the icing sugar. Allow to melt, mixing everything together.
3	Remove from the heat and add the water, a spoonful at a time. If the icing isn't smooth, put back over the heat and stir again. Leave to cool (not too much, or it won't spread easily).	4	Spread in a fairly thick layer over the cake using a palette knife. Take care not to leave any fingerprints, because this icing does not set completely.

SIMPLE CAKES

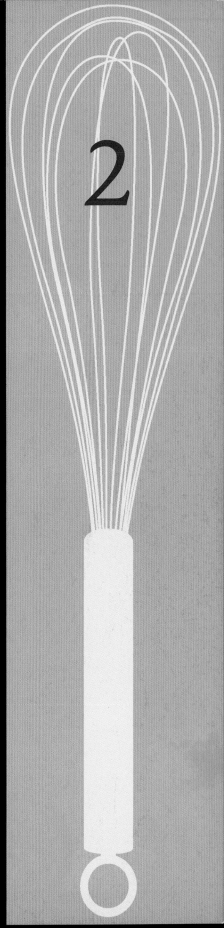

CLASSIC CAKES

Yogurt cake 17
Butter cake 18
Marbled cake 19

CHOCOLATE CAKES

Chocolate fondants 20
Flour-free chocolate cake 21
Brownies 22
Chocolate truffle cake 23

MADE IN THE U.S.A.

Carrot cake 24
Banana & walnut bread 25
Gingerbread 26
Corn bread 27

YOGURT CAKE

❖ **SERVES 8** • PREPARATION: 15 MINUTES • COOKING: 50 MINUTES ❖

3 eggs
125 ml (1 pot, 4 fl oz) natural yogurt
125 ml (1 pot, 4 fl oz) sunflower oil
+ extra for greasing
250 g (2 pots, 8 oz) sugar

2 tablespoons lemon juice
250 g (3 pots, 8 oz) plain flour
1 teaspoon (½ sachet) baking powder
pinch of salt

IN ADVANCE:
Preheat the oven to 180°C (350°F),
Gas Mark 4. Lightly oil a 23-cm (9-in)
nonstick cake tin.

1	Break the eggs into a large bowl and beat well.	2	Whisk in the yogurt.	3	Pour in the oil and whisk again to combine.
4	Add in the sugar, continuing to whisk, then finally the lemon juice.	5	Mix together the flour, baking powder and salt. Add to the liquid mixture and whisk again.	6	Pour the mixture into the prepared cake tin and bake for 50 minutes. Turn out onto a wire rack to cool.

BUTTER CAKE

❧ **SERVES 8–10** • PREPARATION: 25 MINUTES • COOKING: 50 MINUTES ❧

225 g (7½ oz) softened butter + extra
for greasing
275 g (9 oz) sugar
3 eggs + 3 egg yolks

1 teaspoon vanilla extract
1½ teaspoons water
1 teaspoon salt
175 g (6 oz) self-raising flour

IN ADVANCE:
Preheat the oven to 160°C (325°F), Gas
Mark 3 and put a shelf in the centre of the
oven. Thoroughly grease a savarin tin and
place in the fridge.

| 1 | Use an electric whisk to beat the butter until really smooth (about 15 seconds). | 2 | Keep whisking while you slowly sprinkle the sugar over the butter (this should take about 30 seconds). Beat for 4–5 minutes until the butter is almost white. | |
| 3 | Mix the eggs and the yolks with the vanilla extract and the water in a bowl with a pouring lip. | 4 | Very slowly pour the egg mixture over the butter while beating at medium speed. Add the salt and beat again. | ➤ |

5	Add in one third of the flour and incorporate with a flexible spatula then add in the remaining flour, in two batches, making sure the flour is incorporated before adding in the next batch.	Pour the mixture into the prepared tin and smooth the surface with the back of a spoon. Bake for 50 minutes.

6 | Leave in the tin for 5 minutes before turning out the cake onto a plate, then leave to cool on a wire rack.

☞ To ensure the mixture has a good even texture, use eggs at room temperature. If you keep your eggs in the fridge, plunge them into a bowl of hot water for several minutes before using. Don't despair if your mixture looks curdled (as in photo 5), the final result will not be affected!

MARBLED CAKE

❖ **SERVES 8** • PREPARATION: 30 MINUTES • COOKING: 1 HOUR 5 MINUTES ❖

200 g (7 oz) butter + extra for greasing
4 eggs
200 g (7 oz) sugar
1 teaspoon salt

200 g (7 oz) self-raising flour
15 g (½ oz) or 2 sachets vanilla sugar
25 g (1 oz) cocoa powder

IN ADVANCE:
Preheat the oven to 180°C (350°F), Gas
Mark 4 and put a shelf in the centre of the
oven. Grease a 28-cm (11-in) long loaf tin.

1 2
3 4

1	Melt the butter in a saucepan then remove immediately from the heat.	2	Separate the eggs into two large bowls.	
3	Add the sugar and the salt to the egg yolks. Mix thoroughly with a wooden spoon.	4	Add alternately small amounts of flour and melted butter, beating between each addition.	➤

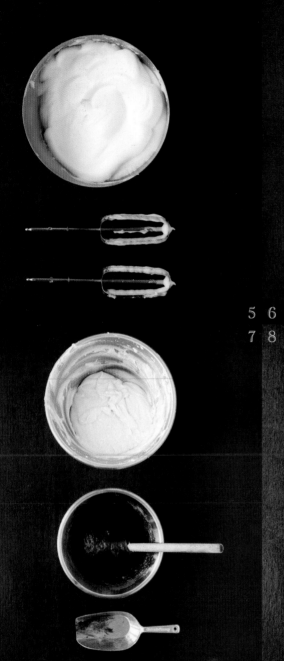

5	Whisk the egg whites into a meringue, adding half the vanilla sugar halfway through.	6	Add the egg whites to the mixture and work in with a wooden spoon.
7	Divide the mixture between two bowls. Add the cocoa powder to one bowl and the remaining vanilla sugar to the other.	8	Using a dessertspoon, spoon the two mixtures alternately into the loaf tin to create a marbled effect.

9

Transfer the tin to the oven and bake for 1 hour. Insert the tip of a sharp knife into the centre of the cake to check it is cooked; the knife should come out clean.

TIP
❋

In most recipes that call for whisked egg whites, the whites have to be delicately incorporated in the mixture, otherwise they break down. For this recipe, though, you don't have to be so careful when you add the whites because the final texture of the cake is more dense.

CHOCOLATE FONDANTS

❖ **SERVES 4** • PREPARATION: 15 MINUTES • COOKING: 15–18 MINUTES ❖

125 g (4 oz) butter
125 g (4 oz) chocolate
4 eggs

125 g (4 oz) sugar
50 g (2 oz) self-raising flour

IN ADVANCE:
Preheat the oven to 180°C (350°F),
Gas Mark 4 and put a shelf in the centre
of the oven.

1	Cut the butter into pieces and put into a small saucepan. Break the chocolate into pieces and place on top of the butter.	2	Put over a low heat and stir with a flexible spatula as soon as the butter starts to melt.
3	As soon as the mixture is smooth, remove from the heat.	4	Break the eggs into a bowl with a pouring lip and beat with the sugar until you have a smooth mixture (about 10 seconds). ➤

5

6 7

5	Pour the melted chocolate over the eggs and mix as lightly as possible using a balloon whisk.	6	Add the flour in three lots, mixing with a flexible spatula between each addition.
		7	Use the mixture to fill 4 ramekins or pots 7 cm (3½ in) diameter with sides 5 cm (2 in) tall. Transfer to the oven for 15–18 minutes.

IS IT COOKED? ❋	TIP ❋
Shake one ramekin while still in the oven; the centre should barely wobble. Note that the cooking time will depend on the size and thickness of your dishes.	☛ You can prepare this dessert in advance. Cover each filled ramekin with cling film and place in the fridge until you are ready to cook. Remove the cling film and bake for 17–20 minutes straight from the fridge.

FLOUR-FREE CHOCOLATE CAKE

❧ MAKES 8 • PREPARATION: 20 MINUTES • COOKING: 25 MINUTES ❧

5 eggs
175 g (6 oz) sugar
225 g (7½ oz) butter + extra for greasing

200 g (7 oz) plain dark chocolate
(minimum 70% cocoa solids)
75 g (3 oz) ground almonds, sieved

IN ADVANCE:
Preheat the oven to 180°C (350°F), Gas
Mark 4 and put a shelf in the centre of the
oven. Grease a 23-cm (9-in) square cake tin
and place in the fridge.

1	Beat the eggs in a large bowl, just enough to break the yolks, then add the sugar. Combine the mixture with a whisk, stopping as soon as it is evenly blended.	2	Put the butter and the chocolate in a saucepan over a medium heat. When the butter has melted, turn off the heat and stir with a flexible spatula until the chocolate has also melted.
3	Pour the chocolate over the eggs and very lightly mix with the whisk. Add the ground almonds and mix again.	4	Pour the mixture into the tin, and give it a tap on the work surface to release any air bubbles. Transfer to the oven for 25 minutes maximum.

BROWNIES

❧ **SERVES 8–10** • PREPARATION: 20 MINUTES • RESTING: 10 MINUTES • COOKING: 35 MINUTES ❧

125 g (4 oz) walnuts
200 g (7 oz) butter + extra for greasing
125 g (4 oz) plain dark chocolate
(minimum 70% cocoa solids)
200 g (7 oz) sugar

4 eggs
¼ teaspoon vanilla extract
150 g (5 oz) self-raising flour
pinch of salt

IN ADVANCE:
Preheat the oven to 180°C (350°F), Gas
Mark 4 and put a shelf in the centre of the
oven. Grease a 23-cm (9-in) square cake
tin. Cut the butter and chocolate into pieces.

1	Roughly chop the walnuts with a knife or break them with your fingers.	2	Put the butter in a saucepan then put the chocolate on top.	3	Place over a gentle heat and stir with a flexible spatula until the butter melts.
4	Add the sugar and mix for 2 minutes (the sugar will not completely dissolve). Remove from the heat.	5	Pour the mixture into a bowl, leave for 10 minutes to cool, then add the eggs, one at a time, whisking well.	6	Add the vanilla extract and whisk once more.

7 8
9 10

7	Mix together the flour and the salt in another bowl. Tip it onto the melted chocolate.	8	Work in the flour with a flexible spatula until it is completely incorporated.
9	Lastly, add the walnuts and mix again.	10	Pour the mixture into the prepared tin. Transfer to the oven for 20–25 minutes. When it is cooked, leave to cool on a wire rack.

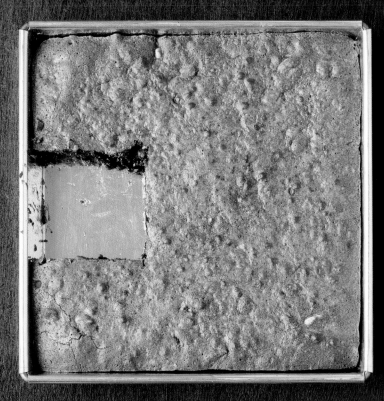

IS IT COOKED?	STORAGE
When cooked, the brownie should not move if you shake the tin but the blade of a knife inserted into the centre will not come out clean.	Cut the brownies into 6-cm (2½-in) squares. You can wrap them individually in cling film if you don't want to eat them immediately. This way, they will keep up to 4 days in the fridge.

CHOCOLATE TRUFFLE CAKE

❧ SERVES 6 • PREPARATION: 15 MINUTES • COOKING: 35 MINUTES ❧

3 eggs
150 g (5 oz) sugar
140 ml (scant ¼ pint) water
200 g (7 oz) plain dark chocolate
(minimum 52% cocoa solids)

135 g (4½ oz) butter
25 g (1 oz) plain flour
cocoa powder, for dusting

IN ADVANCE:
Preheat the oven to 180°C (350°F), Gas
Mark 4 and put a shelf in the centre of the
oven (see page 71). Grease a 23-cm (9-in)
cake tin and line the base with baking paper.

1	Break the eggs into a bowl, beat well and set aside.	2	Put the sugar and water in a saucepan over a medium heat and whisk to dissolve the sugar.	3	When the sugar has dissolved, bring to the boil then remove immediately from the heat.	
4	Add the chocolate in pieces and mix until it has melted.	5	Next add the butter, in cubes, and mix until it is fully incorporated.	6	After 5 minutes, add the beaten eggs.	➢

7 8
9 10

7	Sprinkle the flour over the chocolate mixture and incorporate it with the whisk.	8	Pour the mixture into the prepared tin and transfer to the oven. Bake the cake for 30 minutes or until the centre no longer wobbles.
9	Remove the cake and allow to cool on a wire rack for 5 minutes before turning out onto a plate.	10	When the cake is completely cold, wrap in cling film.

| 11 | Put the cake into the fridge until you are ready to serve (it is best very cold). To decorate, dust with cocoa powder just before serving. | **COOKING IN THE OVEN WITH A BAIN-MARIE**
❄
☛ When you preheat the oven, place in a second shelf under the first. Place a shallow heatproof dish on this shelf and, just before putting the cake into the oven, fill the dish with hot water. |

CARROT CAKE

❧ **SERVES 8** • PREPARATION: 20 MINUTES • COOKING: 55 MINUTES ❧

175 g (6 oz) plain flour
1 teaspoon each bicarbonate of soda, baking powder, salt, ground cinnamon, mixed spice
3 eggs
200 g (7 oz) sugar

150 ml (¼ pint) sunflower oil
65 g (2½ oz) apple purée
225 g (7½ oz) grated carrots
50 g (2 oz) walnuts, roughly chopped
50 g (2 oz) raisins

IN ADVANCE:
Preheat the oven to 180°C (350°F), Gas Mark 4 and put a shelf in the centre of the oven with a baking sheet on it. Grease and line a 28-cm (11-in) long loaf tin.

1	Sift the flour, bicarbonate, baking powder, salt and spices into a large bowl. Make a well in the centre.	2	In a separate bowl, whisk the eggs just enough to break the yolks.	3	Add the sugar and whisk until thick and creamy.
4	Pour in the oil in a steady stream, whisking as if making mayonnaise.	5	Next add the apple purée.	6	Pour the mixture into the well in the middle of the flour. ➤

| 7 | Stir the mixture using a flexible spatula and add in the grated carrot, walnuts and raisins. Continue to work the mixture until it is blended evenly. Transfer the mixture to the prepared loaf tin. | **TIP** ❈

☛ To remove any air bubbles and settle the mixture in the tin, give it a gentle tap on the work surface before cooking. |

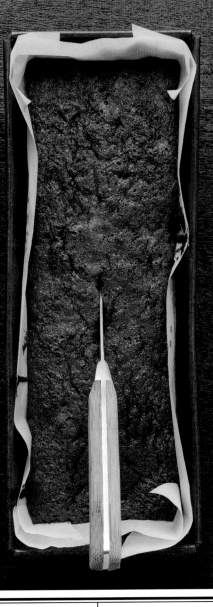

8

Bake the cake for 55 minutes on the prepared baking sheet. When it is cooked, run the blade of a knife around the sides. Leave it to stand for 15 minutes before turning out onto a wire rack. Allow to cool completely before icing (see next page). To serve, cut the cake into 2-cm (1-in) slices.

IS IT COOKED?

☞ When the cake is cooked it will be a dark reddish-brown. The tip of a sharp knife inserted into the centre of the cake should come out completely clean.

CARROT CAKE ICING

❧ **MAKES 150 G (5 OZ)** • PREPARATION: 10 MINUTES ❧

25 g (1 oz) butter
50 g (2 oz) cream cheese
½ teaspoon lemon juice

¼ teaspoon vanilla extract
65 g (2½ oz) icing sugar

IN ADVANCE:
Cut the butter into pieces and work into a pomade.

1 2
3 4

1	Using a wooden spatula, work the butter and the cream cheese together until they are completely smooth.	2	Transfer to the bowl of a food processor, add the lemon juice and vanilla extract and mix for no more than 5 seconds. Scrape the sides of the bowl with a spatula.
3	Add the icing sugar and mix again for no more than 10 seconds until the mixture is creamy.	4	Cover with cling film and keep for up to 4 days in the fridge. Spread over the carrot cake just before serving.

BANANA & WALNUT BREAD

SERVES 8–10 • PREPARATION: 25 MINUTES • COOKING: 50 MINUTES TO 1 HOUR

150 g (5 oz) softened butter
150 g (5 oz) sugar
3 eggs at room temperature
4 bananas

2 teaspoons vanilla extract
75 g (3 oz) walnuts
325 g (11 oz) plain flour
2 teaspoons baking powder

IN ADVANCE:
Preheat the oven to 160°C (325°F), Gas Mark 3. Grease a savarin mould or use a nonstick one.

1 2
3 4

1	Beat the butter for 15 seconds using an electric beater then add the sugar.	2	Continue to beat for several minutes until the mixture is pale, light and fluffy.	
3	Beat the eggs well in a bowl, preferably one with a pouring lip, and pour them very slowly on the butter–sugar mixture while continuing to beat at medium speed.	4	Crush the bananas with a fork and add them, along with the vanilla extract. Work them in using a hand whisk.	➤

5 Roughly chop the walnuts and put them in a bowl. Add the flour and baking powder and mix everything together.

Incorporate the dry ingredients into the banana mixture and work everything together smoothly using a flexible spatula.

| 6 | Pour the mixture into the cake tin and place it on a baking sheet. Transfer to the oven and bake for 50 minutes to 1 hour. When the cake is cooked, leave it in the tin for 15 minutes before turning out. Enjoy it as it is, cut into medium slices, or with butter and jam. | **OPTION**
❋
You can also use a classic loaf tin (28 cm/11 in), and bake it at 180°C (350°F), Gas Mark 4. Whichever shape cake tin you use, the cooking test is the same: insert the blade of a sharp pointed knife right into the centre of the cake; it should come out clean. |

GINGERBREAD

⇢ **SERVES 8–10** • PREPARATION: 14 MINUTES • COOKING: 1 HOUR ⇠

300 g (10 oz) plain flour + pinch of salt
1 teaspoon each bicarbonate of soda,
ground ginger, mixed spice
½ teaspoon each ground cinnamon, grated
nutmeg, cocoa powder

100 g (3½ oz) butter + extra for greasing
230 ml (7½ fl oz) maple syrup
150 g (5 oz) sugar
100 ml (3½ fl oz) cultured buttermilk
100 ml (3½ fl oz) milk + 1 egg

IN ADVANCE:
Preheat the oven to 180°C (350°F),
Gas Mark 4. Ensure the liquid ingredients
and the egg are all at room temperature.
Melt the butter.

1 2
3 4

1	Mix the flour, salt, bicarbonate, spices and cocoa powder in a medium bowl.	2	Put the melted butter, maple syrup, sugar, buttermilk, milk and the egg in a separate, large bowl.	
3	Thoroughly mix the liquid ingredients using an electric whisk on slow speed.	4	Add the dry ingredients and whisk at medium speed until the mixture is smooth and evenly blended.	➤

5	Thoroughly grease a 28-cm (11-in) long loaf tin or mould. Pour the mixture into the tin, transfer to the oven and bake for 55 minutes.	**TIP** ✸
		☛ To ensure the cake doesn't burn, stand the tin on a baking sheet.

6	Remove the cake from the oven and allow to cool for 10 minutes before turning out onto a wire rack. Once it has cooled to room temperature, wrap in cling film.	Enjoy warm or at room temperature, as it is or with a little crème fraîche or whipped cream. This cake will keep for up to 5 days if wrapped in cling film and stored at room temperature.

CORN BREAD

❧ **SERVES 8** • PREPARATION: 15 MINUTES • COOKING: 30 MINUTES ❧

30 g (generous 1 oz) melted butter + extra
for greasing
150 g (5 oz) polenta (cornmeal), see page 89
150 g (5 oz) plain flour
2 teaspoons baking powder

1 teaspoon bicarbonate of soda
25 g (1 oz) sugar + 1 teaspoon salt
2 eggs
150 ml (¼ pint) milk
150 ml (¼ pint) cultured buttermilk

IN ADVANCE:
Preheat the oven to 220°C (425°F), Gas
Mark 7 and put a shelf in the centre of the
oven. Grease a 28-cm (11-in) long loaf tin
or an 18-cm (7-in) square cake tin.

1 2
3 4

1	Melt the butter in a small saucepan. Remove immediately from the heat.	2	Put the polenta, flour, baking powder, bicarbonate, sugar and salt in a large bowl.	
3	Mix all the dry ingredients together and make a well in the centre.	4	Break the eggs into the well and mix in gently using a wooden spoon.	➤

5 6
7 8

5	Add the milk and buttermilk. Mix well until the dry ingredients are fully incorporated.	6	Pour in the melted butter and mix again until everything is evenly blended.
7	Pour the mixture into the tin. Transfer to the oven and bake for 30 minutes.	8	When the top is golden brown, remove the cake from the oven and turn out onto a wire rack to cool for 5–10 minutes.

	TO SERVE ❋	TO REHEAT ❋
9	Serve cut into small squares or slices. Enjoy warm, with a knob of butter. You can eat it on its own, as a cake, or as an accompaniment to savoury dishes (with soup or vegetable dishes, for example).	Cover the bread if not serving immediately. Reheat for 5–10 minutes at 180°C (350°F), Gas Mark 4.
		NOTE ❋
		Many brands of polenta are precooked. You can use this type in the recipe, but the result will turn out a little drier.

LAYERED CAKES

3

CHOUX PASTRY

Choux pastry 28
Praline choux 29
Caramel topping 30
Profiteroles 31
Chocolate éclairs 32
Choux puffs 33
Rose St-Honoré choux 34

PUFF PASTRY

Puff pastry 35
Mille-feuilles 36
Kings' cake 37

CHEESECAKES

Tiramisu 38
Mascarpone cheesecake 39
Corsican cheesecake 40

FILLED CAKES

Swiss roll 41
Coffee log 42
Poppyseed cake 43
Chocolate charlotte 44
Vacherin 45

CHOUX PASTRY

❖ **MAKES 300 G (10 OZ) • PREPARATION: 20 MINUTES • COOKING: 15–20 MINUTES** ❖

2 eggs
125 ml (4 fl oz) water
50 g (2 oz) butter, cut into small dice
½ teaspoon salt
75 g (3 oz) self-raising flour

IN ADVANCE:
Preheat the oven to 220°C (425°F),
Gas Mark 7 and put a shelf in the centre
of the oven. Line a baking sheet with
baking paper.

Break the eggs into a bowl, beat well and
set aside.

1	Put the water, butter and salt in a saucepan over a medium heat just long enough to melt the butter.	2	Bring to a rolling boil. Immediately remove from the heat and place on a pan stand. Add the flour in one go.	
3	Mix with a wooden spoon until it leaves the sides of the pan and makes a ball of dough.	4	Stir in half the beaten eggs and incorporate thoroughly before adding the rest.	➤

5	Put the dough immediately into a piping bag, or use a freezer bag and snip one corner. Pipe out small buns on the baking sheet, spaced well apart to allow them to expand and for the hot air to circulate as they bake.

HOW TO MAKE THE CHOUX
❊

☛ Hold the filled piping bag perpendicular, a few centimetres above the baking sheet. Squeeze out the dough, keeping the bag perpendicular all the time.

6	Transfer the choux to the oven and bake for 10 minutes, then wedge open the oven door with a wooden spoon and bake for a further 5 minutes. Allow to cool on a wire rack.	**FOR LIGHT AND PUFFY CHOUX** ✻ Just before putting the choux in the oven, prick them lightly with the wetted tines of a fork. This gives them an even shape and helps them to puff up as they cook. Wait until the choux are lightly coloured before opening the oven door.

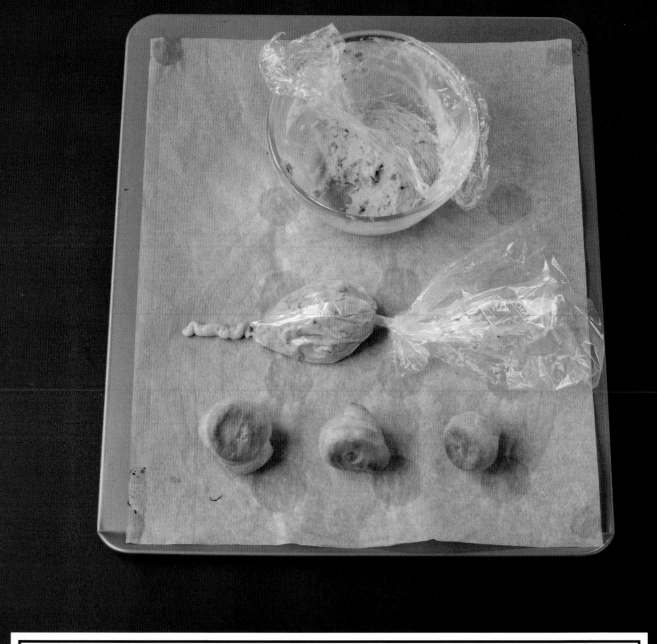

PRALINE CHOUX

ENOUGH FOR 25 CHOUX
❊

Prepare 700 g (1 lb 8 oz) praline-flavoured Confectioner's Cream (see recipe 02) and 25 choux.

Fill a piping bag with the prepared cream. Pierce the base of each bun with the tip of a sharp knife and

insert the nozzle. Squeeze the bag to fill each bun with cream. Place the filled buns upright again.

CARAMEL TOPPING

ENOUGH FOR 25 CHOUX

Once you have filled the choux buns, make 100 g (3½ oz) of Caramel (see recipe 09).

Stop cooking it before it darkens too much (the caramel will continue to colour off the heat).

Immediately dip the top of each bun into the caramel then place them on a cooling rack.

PROFITEROLES

❊ **MAKES 20 CHOUX** • PREPARATION: 10 MINUTES • COOKING: 5 MINUTES ❊

20 choux made with 300 g (10 oz) Choux
Pastry (see recipe 28)
500 ml (17 fl oz) vanilla ice cream

CHOCOLATE SAUCE:
100 g (3½ oz) chocolate
90 ml (3¼ fl oz) milk
100 ml (3½ fl oz) single cream

IN ADVANCE:
Allow the choux buns to cool slightly then
slice off the top third with a serrated knife.
Take the ice cream out of the freezer. Break
the chocolate into pieces.

1	To make the chocolate sauce, pour the milk and cream into a small saucepan and bring to the boil.	2	Remove from the heat, add the chocolate, and stir until smooth. Return to the heat and allow to bubble gently then remove and set aside.
3	Use a teaspoon to fill the sliced choux buns generously with the softened ice cream, allowing it to overspill a little. Replace the tops.	4	Pour a little hot chocolate sauce into the base of small serving dishes. Place 2 profiteroles in each dish and serve with extra chocolate sauce.

CHOCOLATE ÉCLAIRS

⇥ MAKES 20 • PREPARATION: 10 MINUTES • COOKING: 5 MINUTES ⇤

20 éclairs, 10-cm (4-in) long, made with
300 g (10 oz) Choux Pastry (see recipe 28)
700 g (1 lb 8 oz) Confectioner's Cream
flavoured with chocolate (see recipe 02)

CHOCOLATE ICING:
100 g (3½ oz) plain dark chocolate
75 g (3 oz) icing sugar
40 g (1½ oz) butter
3 tablespoons water

IN ADVANCE:
Slit the éclairs down one side with a
serrated knife and fill them with the
confectioner's cream using a piping bag.

| 1 | To make the icing, melt the chocolate in a saucepan over a very low heat (or in a bain-marie). Stir with a flexible spatula. | 2 | Keep the pan over a very low heat, add the icing sugar and the butter, cut into dice. Allow to melt, stirring all the time. Remove from the heat and add the water, a spoonful at a time. |
| 3 | Allow the icing to cool slightly: too hot and it will run; too cold and it will not spread easily. | 4 | Place the filled éclairs on a rack and spread each one with a thickish layer of icing using a palette knife. |

CHOUX PUFFS

➤ **MAKES 25** • **PREPARATION: 20 MINUTES** • **COOKING: 14 MINUTES** ⬤

CHOUX PASTRY:
125 ml (4 fl oz) water
50 g (2 oz) butter, cut into pieces
½ teaspoon salt

1 teaspoon sugar
75 g (3 oz) self-raising flour
2 eggs
sugar nibs (large grain sugar), to decorate

IN ADVANCE:
Preheat the oven to 200°C (400°F),
Gas Mark 6.

1

Prepare the choux pastry, following the method given in recipe 28, by heating the water, butter, salt and sugar. Add the flour and eggs as described in steps 3 and 4.

Pipe out mini choux buns, spaced well apart, on a baking sheet. Sprinkle them with the sugar nibs.

Transfer the sheet to the oven and bake for 15 minutes, then prop open the oven door with a wooden spoon and bake for a further 5 minutes. Remove the buns from the oven and allow to cool on the baking sheet.

ROSE ST-HONORÉ CHOUX

❖ **MAKES 4** • PREPARATION: 20 MINUTES • COOKING: 15–20 MINUTES ❖

300g (10 oz) Choux Pastry (see recipe 28)
350 g (12 oz) Confectioner's Cream
(see recipe 02), mixed with ¼ teaspoon
rose water

225 g (8 oz) Chantilly Cream (see recipe 14),
mixed with 2 drops of pink food colouring
100g (3½ oz) Plain Icing (see recipe 15),
mixed with 2 drops of pink food colouring

IN ADVANCE:
Cover a baking sheet with baking paper.
Preheat the oven to 220°C (425°F), Gas
Mark 7. Prepare the Confectioner's Cream,
adding the rose water with the milk.

1	Pipe 4 crowns and 12 mini choux on the sheet. Bake for 10–15 minutes. Prop open the oven door with a wooden spoon, bake for 5 minutes.	3	Prepare the plain icing (see recipe 15), adding in the food colouring at the end.
2	Remove from the oven, leave for 10 minutes then place the choux on a wire rack. Cut each crown in two across the middle with a serrated knife, and pierce the base of the mini choux.		➤

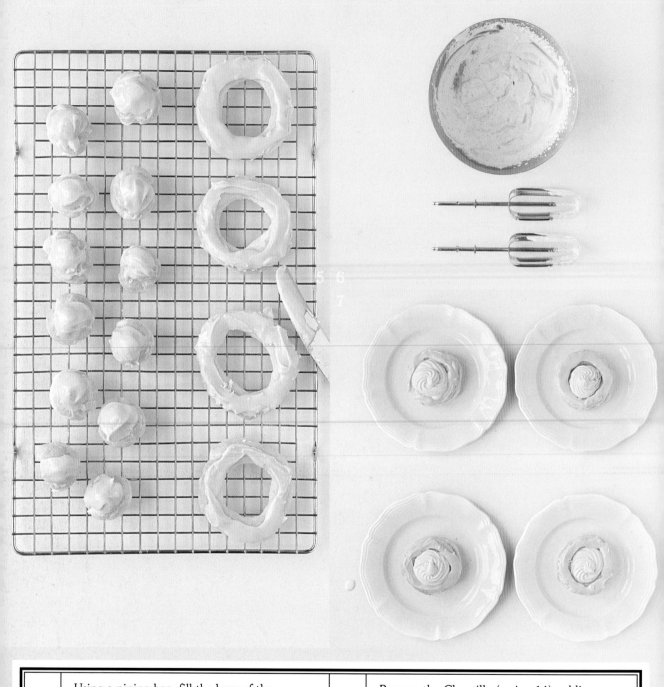

| 5 | Using a piping bag, fill the base of the 4 crowns with confectioner's cream then replace the tops. Then fill the bases of the mini choux. Ice the tops of the mini choux and the filled crowns using a fine-bladed spatula (or a smooth-bladed knife). | 6 | Prepare the Chantilly (recipe 14), adding in the food colouring with the cream at the outset. |
| | | 7 | Arrange the filled crowns on plates and top each one with Chantilly. Place the mini choux on the crowns. |

8	Serve immediately (or keep in a cool place for no more than 1 hour before serving).

OPTION
— ❋ —

For a stronger rose flavour, add ¼ teaspoon rose water to the cream before whipping the Chantilly.

TO SIMPLIFY THE TASK OF ICING
— ❋ —

You can make the plain icing more liquid by adding a few extra drops of lemon juice then simply dip the top of each crown and mini choux in the icing.

PUFF PASTRY

✦ **MAKES 900 G (ABOUT 1 LB 12 OZ)** • PREPARATION: 30 MINUTES • REFRIGERATION: 2 HOURS ✦

420 g (14 oz) plain flour
325 g (11 oz) butter, diced
150 ml (¼ pint) very cold water

3 teaspoons sugar
½ teaspoon salt

IN ADVANCE:
Sift the flour onto the work surface and scatter the diced butter on top.

1	Rub the butter into the flour until it forms crumbs. Make a well in the centre and pour in the water.	**2**	Add the sugar and salt and dissolve in the water using your fingertips. Work in the crumb mixture.
3	You will have a lumpy batter in the middle. Bring all the crumb mixture into this batter.		
4	When the dough forms, press down bit by bit using the palm of your hand.	**5**	Bring to a fairly uneven whole, press down once and make it into a ball.
6	Shape into a block, wrap in cling film and refrigerate for 1 hour.	➤	

7	Remove the pastry from the fridge and place on a lightly floured work surface. Put a rolling pin on the pastry.	8	Roll out to form a rectangle measuring approximately 40 x 25 cm (16 x 10 in).	9	Fold a third of the pastry along its long side into the centre then fold the other long side on top.
10	Now do the same with the short side, folding the pastry in on itself.	11	Lightly press down using the palm of your hand.	12	Roll out again to form a rectangle measuring about 40 x 25 cm (16 x 10 in).

13 14
15 16

13	Repeat these steps: flour the work surface again and roll out the pastry to make a rectangle measuring 40 x 25 cm (16 x 10 in).	14	Fold again into three as in step 9.
15	Now fold into three on itself on the short side as in step 10.	16	If you only need half the pastry, flatten it into a rectangle measuring 20 x 10 cm (8 x 4 in) and cut in two (you can freeze one half). Refrigerate the pastry for 1 hour before use.

MILLE-FEUILLES

❧ MAKES 4 • PREPARATION: 25 MINUTES • COOKING: 15 MINUTES ❧

350 g (12 oz) Confectioner's Cream (see recipe 02)
50 g (2 oz) Chantilly Cream (see recipe 14)
450 g (14½ oz) Puff Pastry (see recipe 35)
10 g (scant ½ oz) icing sugar

IN ADVANCE:
Prepare the confectioner's cream, not too thick, and put in the fridge.

Preheat the oven to 220°C (425°F), Gas Mark 7. Line a baking sheet with baking paper.

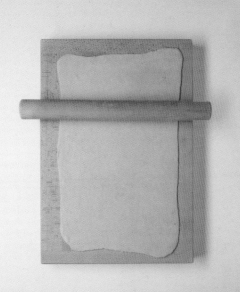

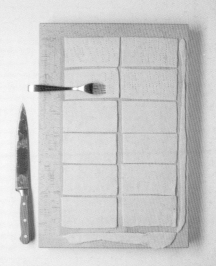

1	Remove the chilled confectioner's cream from the fridge and incorporate the Chantilly, a spoonful at a time.	2	Cover with cling film and return to the fridge.	
3	Thinly roll out the pastry to a rectangle the size of your baking sheet and about 2–3 mm (⅛ in) thick.	4	Cut the pastry into 12 neat rectangles (trim off the edges) using a sharp knife. Prick each rectangle with the tines of a small fork.	➤

5 6
7 8

5	Place half the rectangles on the baking sheet (and the rest in the fridge) and bake for 10 minutes (they should not be too brown). Bake the second batch in the same way.	6	Preheat the grill. Select 4 rectangles, turn them with the underside (non-risen) face up, sprinkle with the icing sugar and flash them under the hot grill for 1 minute to caramelize.
7	Spread a layer of confectioner's cream on the remaining rectangles.	8	Build up the rectangles in twos then top with the caramelized slice.

9 Serve the mille-feuilles as soon as possible, so that the cream doesn't have time to soak into the pastry layers.

SERVING OPTION
❄
You can also present this as a cake, trimming up the sides first, before cutting into slices.

VARIATION
❄
For a very light cream filling, increase the proportion of Chantilly to confectioner's cream.

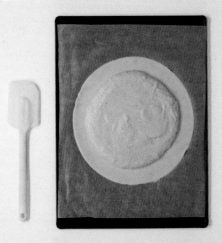

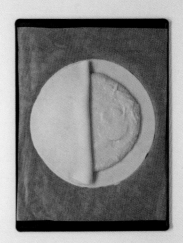

5 6
7 8

5	Spread the almond cream mixture over the first circle of pastry, stopping 3 cm (a good inch) short of the edges.	6	Cover with the second pastry circle, pressing firmly to seal the edges all round.
7	Glaze the top of the galette all over with the beaten egg. Use a knife to draw arcs of a circle over the top, working from the centre out.	8	Use the knife to make small nicks all round the edge of the galette. Make small holes (and a larger one in the centre) over the surface to allow the air to escape. Chill for 30 minutes.

9

Transfer the galette to the very hot oven. When it has risen well (about 15 minutes), reduce the temperature to 200°C (400°F), Gas Mark 6. Continue to bake for about a further 20 minutes. Serve warm or at room temperature.

FREEZING ADVICE
❋

You can put the uncooked galette on a plate (without glazing or decorating it). Allow to harden in the freezer for 12 hours before popping it into a freezer bag. Seal well. When you are ready to bake it, glaze and decorate the galette before putting it in the oven still frozen. Allow a further 10 minutes' cooking time.

TIRAMISU

☞ SERVES 6–8 • PREPARATION: 25 MINUTES • SETTING: 6 HOURS ☜

250 ml (8 fl oz) freshly made strong coffee
65 g (2½ oz) sugar
5 eggs
500 g (1 lb) mascarpone

300 g (10 oz) Savoy or ladyfinger biscuits,
about 35 biscuits
2 tablespoons cocoa powder

IN ADVANCE:
Pour the hot coffee into a bowl. Add
1 teaspoonful of the sugar, mix and
allow to cool.

1 2
3 4

1	Separate the eggs. Beat the yolks with the remaining sugar until the mixture turns pale and creamy.	2	Add the mascarpone and beat with an electric beater until the mixture is light and fluffy.	
3	Whisk the egg whites to a supple, not too firm, meringue.	4	Add the whites in two goes into the cream mixture, working them in with a flexible spatula.	➤

5
6

| 5 | Very quickly dip several biscuits, one by one, in the coffee and, before they lose their shape, use them to line the base of a large square dish or mould in a single layer. | 6 | Cover with a thin layer of the cream mixture. Build up two more layers of biscuits and cream in this way. Cover the dish with cling film and refrigerate for at least 6 hours. |

		TIP ✳
7	Just before serving, sift the cocoa powder through a small strainer over the tiramisu.	The biscuits become over soft if you leave them too long in the coffee. If you wish, you can use boudoir biscuits instead. You will need to leave them a little longer in the coffee to soften.

MASCARPONE CHEESECAKE

✦ **SERVES 10–12** • PREPARATION: 20 MINUTES • COOKING: 1 HOUR 15 MINUTES • RESTING: 3 HOURS MINIMUM ✦

FOR THE BASE:
125 g (4 oz) plain biscuits (such as digestives)
75 g (3 oz) butter
40g (1½ oz) sugar

FOR THE TOPPING:
400 g (13 oz) cream cheese
220 g (7¼ oz) sugar
200 g (7 oz) mascarpone
3 eggs + 1 teaspoon vanilla extract

IN ADVANCE:
Preheat the oven to 150°C (300°F), Gas Mark 2. Put a shelf in the centre with a second just below and place a shallow dish or deep plate on this lower shelf.

1	Whiz the biscuits for 30–60 seconds in the bowl of a mixer fitted with a blade to make fine crumbs.	2	Melt the butter in a small saucepan and remove from the heat.	3	Mix the sugar with the biscuit crumbs in a bowl.	
4	Pour the melted butter on top and mix together with a fork.	5	Spread this mixture in the base of a 20-cm (8-in) springform cake tin.	6	Firm the crumbs then refrigerate the tin for 5–10 minutes.	➤

7 8
9 10

7	Put the cream cheese with the sugar in the bowl of a food processor fitted with a blade. Mix for 1 minute until the mixture is softened.	8	Add the mascarpone and mix again for 10–20 seconds. Remove the lid and scrape down the sides with a flexible spatula.
9	Add the eggs one at a time, mixing well before adding the next. Scrape down the sides again then add the vanilla extract and mix briefly.	10	Remove the tin from the fridge and pour the cream mixture over the biscuit base.

| 11 | Fill the shallow dish or bowl on the lower oven shelf with very hot water. Transfer the cheesecake to the upper shelf of the oven. Bake for 1 hour 15 minutes or until the middle of the cheesecake is no longer runny. | **SETTING**
✳
Remove the cheesecake from the oven and allow to cool on a wire rack. Once cool, cover with cling film and allow to set in the fridge for at least 3 hours before serving. It will reach its ideal consistency after 12 hours. |

CORSICAN CHEESECAKE

⇺ SERVES 6–8 • PREPARATION: 20 MINUTES • COOKING: 45 MINUTES ⇸

500 g (1 lb) ricotta or brocciù (ewe's milk cheese) if you can find it
olive oil, for greasing
rind of 1 unwaxed lemon

5 eggs
150g (5 oz) sugar
½ teaspoon eau-de-vie
pinch of salt

IN ADVANCE:
Drain the cheese (if necessary) for 1 hour. Oil a 25-cm (10-in) cake tin. Grate the lemon rind. Preheat the oven to 180°C (350°F), Gas Mark 4.

| 1 | Separate the eggs. | 2 | Whisk the yolks with the sugar, using a hand-held or an electric whisk, until pale. | 3 | Add the ricotta in two lots. Mix in with a hand whisk. Add the lemon rind then the eau-de-vie. |
| 4 | Beat the egg whites with the salt until they form firm peaks. | 5 | Use a flexible spatula to incorporate the whites with the ricotta mixture. | 6 | Do not overmix; use the spatula gently. ➤ |

| 7 | Pour the mixture into the prepared tin and lightly smooth the surface with a spatula. | **TIP**
❋
☛ In this recipe you can incorporate the egg whites with less concern for them flattening because this mixture does not need to be too light and fluffy. |

8	Transfer the tin to the oven and bake for 45 minutes. Remove and allow to cool on a wire rack. Cover and refrigerate before serving.

TO SERVE
❉

This cheesecake should be served chilled. You can serve it with a red berry compôte or a fresh coulis.

NOTE
❉

This cheesecake originates in Corsica where it is called Fiadone. Brocciù is a soft white cheese made from ewe's milk, and is considered the island's national cheese. If you cannot find it, use ricotta. The cheesecake is flavoured with Mirto, a myrtle-flavoured liqueur, also made in Corsica. You can use an eau-de-vie of your choice.

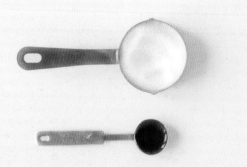

SWISS ROLL

❧ SERVES 8 • PREPARATION: 40 MINUTES • COOKING: 10 MINUTES ❧

SPONGE:
35 g (1½ oz) butter
4 egg yolks + 3 egg whites
75 g (3 oz) sugar + an extra teaspoonful
for the egg whites
75 g (3 oz) self-raising flour

VANILLA SYRUP:
75 ml (3 fl oz) water
50 g (2 oz) sugar
½ teaspoon vanilla extract
250 g (8 oz) strawberry jam

IN ADVANCE:
Preheat the oven to 240°C (475°F),
Gas Mark 9. Line a baking sheet
measuring 40 x 30 cm (16 x 12 in)
with baking paper.

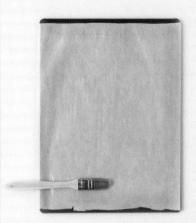

1	Begin by making the sponge cake. Melt the butter in a small saucepan.	2	Using a little of the melted butter, grease the baking paper well.	3	With an electric whisk, beat the egg yolks with the 75 g (3 oz) of sugar for 5 minutes on medium.	
4	Gently incorporate the flour using a flexible spatula; do not overmix.	5	Whisk the egg whites, adding the spoonful of sugar once they start to hold their shape.	6	Add the egg whites and the melted butter to the yolks.	➤

7 8
9 10

7	Gently mix everything together before very carefully pouring the mixture onto the baking sheet – try not to burst the air bubbles.	8	Spread the mixture over the entire sheet using a palette knife.
9	Transfer to the oven and bake for 7 minutes, until the top is lightly coloured.	10	Remove the sponge from the oven and invert it immediately onto a lightly oiled work surface.

11	Peel off the baking paper, cover the sponge with a clean tea towel (this keeps it moist so that it will not break when rolled), and allow to cool.

NOTE
❋

☞ Go easy with the spatula or you will break the air bubbles in the mixture. These are what give the sponge its light texture.

TIP
❋

Spread the sponge mixture with smooth strokes to get it uniformly thick, 4–6 mm (about ¼ inch) maximum. Otherwise, thinner parts will dry out during baking.

➢

12	Pour the water into a small saucepan then add the sugar. Heat gently.	13	Dissolve the sugar, stirring with a whisk, then bring to the boil and remove from the heat immediately.	14	Allow the syrup to cool then add the vanilla extract and mix well.
15	Use a pastry brush to spread the syrup over the sponge cake.	16	Cover with jam, reserving 2 tablespoonfuls, then roll up the sponge tightly.	17	Place the reserved jam in a small pan and gently melt with 1 tablespoon water.

18	Use a pastry brush to cover the Swiss roll completely with the thinned jam.	**STORAGE** ❉ The Swiss roll will keep in the fridge for up to 4 days.

OPTION 1 ❉	**OPTION 2** ❉
Make the sponge in advance and roll it up with its baking paper immediately you take it out of the oven. Wrap in cling film.	You can make a narrower roll (like a log), in which case only cover two-thirds or half of the width of the baking sheet with the sponge mixture.

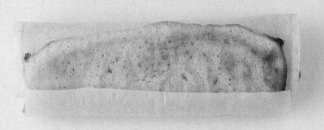

COFFEE LOG

❧ **SERVES 10** • PREPARATION: 20 MINUTES • COOKING: 5 MINUTES • RESTING: 1 HOUR ❦

1 cooked Swiss Roll (see recipe 41) measuring about 20 cm (8 in)
300 g coffee-flavoured Butter Cream (see recipe 03)

COFFEE SYRUP:
50 g (2 oz) sugar
75 g (3 fl oz) water
¼ teaspoon coffee extract

1	Dissolve the sugar in the water over a gentle heat. Bring to the boil, remove from the heat and allow to cool. Mix in the coffee extract.	2	Brush the cooled syrup over the prepared Swiss roll. Spread three-quarters of the butter cream over the sponge.
3	Roll up the sponge as tightly as possible from the smaller side.	4	Cover the log with the remaining cream using a spatula. Refrigerate for 1 hour before serving.

POPPYSEED CAKE

✦ SERVES 12 • PREPARATION: 35 MINUTES • COOKING: 35 MINUTES ✦

25 g (1 oz) raisins
a little rum for soaking
400 g (13 oz) Sweet Shortcrust Pastry (see recipe 66)
50 g (2 oz) butter

400 g (13 oz) poppyseeds
200 g (7 oz) caster sugar
50 g (2 oz) honey
20 g (¾ oz) ground almonds
7 g (¼ oz) or 1 sachet vanilla sugar

rind of 1 lemon
2 egg whites + 1 whole egg, for glazing
IN ADVANCE:
Preheat the oven to 180°C (350°F), Gas Mark 4.

1	Cover the raisins with rum and leave to swell. Butter a 23-cm (9-in) square cake tin, or its rectangular equivalent.	2	Thinly roll out the pastry into two sheets the size of your tin.	
3	Place one sheet in the base of the tin.	4	Melt the butter in a small saucepan. Remove from the heat and set aside.	➤

5	Run the poppyseeds through a coffee grinder in batches and tip them into a large bowl.	6	Add the caster sugar and mix well.	7	Next mix in the melted butter, then add the honey and mix again.
8	Incorporate the ground almonds along with the vanilla sugar.	9	Lastly, add the lemon rind and the drained raisins.	10	Whisk the egg whites until firm and stiff.

11 12
13 14

11	Gently incorporate the whisked whites into the poppyseed mixture.	12	Tip the mixture into the cake tin to cover the pastry base.
13	Place the second sheet of pastry on top. Glaze the pastry with the beaten egg.	14	Bake in the oven for 35 minutes. Serve cut into squares.

5 6
7 8

5	Continue to line the mould with all the biscuits in this way. Leave the base empty.	6	Pour the chocolate mousse into the centre of the dish.
7	Quickly dip the reserved 10 biscuits in the sweetened water and use them to cover the top of the mousse.	8	Place two plates that fit the size of the mould on top of the charlotte. Wrap everything in cling film and refrigerate for 3 hours.

	TO TURN OUT THE CHARLOTTE	**TO SERVE**
9	Unwrap the charlotte and remove the plates. Dip the base of the mould into very hot water, put a serving plate on top and invert the mould. Gently remove the circle of baking paper and serve immediately.	Serve the chocolate charlotte with vanilla custard (see recipe 01), decorated with grated chocolate if you wish.

VACHERIN

→ **SERVES 6** • **PREPARATION: 55 MINUTES** • **COOKING: 1 HOUR 30 MINUTES** • **FREEZING: 2 HOURS** ←

FRENCH MERINGUE:
3 egg whites
the same weight in both caster sugar
and icing sugar (about 100 g/3½ oz of each)
500 ml (17 fl oz) vanilla ice cream

500 ml (17 fl oz) strawberry ice cream
225 g (8 oz) Chantilly Cream (see recipe 14)
fresh fruit, to serve
250 g (8 oz) Red Berry Compôte
(see recipe 13), to serve

IN ADVANCE:
Preheat the oven to 90°C (195°F),
Gas Mark ¼ or to its coolest setting.

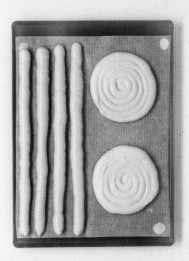

1	To make the meringue, whisk the egg whites in a large bowl. Add the caster sugar once the whites hold their shape.	2	Whisk again until the egg whites are firm. Sift over the icing sugar using a fine sieve and incorporate with a flexible spatula.
3	Draw two circles 12 cm (5 in) in diameter (use a small saucepan as a guide) on baking paper lining a baking sheet. Use a piping bag to fill both circles almost to the edge with meringue.	4	Pipe 4 sticks of meringue next to the spirals. Bake for 1 hour 30 minutes. Take the ice cream from the freezer 10–20 minutes before the end of cooking. ➤

5	Use the same pan that served as a guide for the meringue circles and line the interior with cling film, allowing plenty to overlap the sides.	6	Turn the two ice creams into separate bowls and work with a spoon to soften them.
7	When the meringue has cooled completely, place one disc in the base of the saucepan.	8	Add the softened ice creams and fill almost to the top.

| 9 | Cover the ice cream with the second meringue disc. Place the pan in the freezer and leave to harden for at least 2 hours. | **TIP** ❋ ☞ Be sure to make the meringue discs slightly smaller than the diameter of your saucepan so that you can slip them into it without breaking. Don't make them too small, though: the saucepan serves as a mould for assembling the vacherin and the meringues must be tailored to fit. | ➤ |

LITTLE CAKES

4

FRENCH MERINGUES

❖ **MAKES 250 G (8 OZ) MERINGUE** • PREPARATION: 10 MINUTES • COOKING: 1 HOUR 30 MINUTES TO 2 HOURS ❖

3 egg whites
the same weight in both caster sugar and
icing sugar (about 100 g/3½ oz of each)

IN ADVANCE:
Preheat the oven to 90°C (195°F), Gas Mark
¼ or set to your oven's lowest temperature.
Cover a baking sheet with baking paper.

1 2
3 4

1	Whisk the egg whites in a large bowl. Add the caster sugar once the whites hold their shape.	2	Whisk again until the egg whites are fully firm. Sift over the icing sugar through a fine-mesh sieve and incorporate with a flexible spatula.
3	Drop dessertspoonfuls of meringue on the baking sheet, spaced apart. Transfer to the oven and bake for 1 hour 30 minutes to 2 hours.	4	Once cooked, switch off the oven and leave the meringues inside to cool, with the door closed. They will easily peel off the paper.

BLUEBERRY MUFFINS

☙ MAKES 6 MUFFINS • PREPARATION: 15 MINUTES • COOKING: 25 MINUTES ☙

25 g (1 oz) butter
1 egg
75 g (3 oz) sugar
150 ml (¼ pint) crème fraîche or
soured cream

125 g (4 oz) flour
½ teaspoon salt
1 teaspoon baking powder
75 g (3 oz) frozen blueberries

IN ADVANCE:
Preheat the oven to 180°C (350°F),
Gas Mark 4. Grease 6 individual muffin
tins or a 6-hole tray.

1
2

| 1 | Melt the butter then remove from the heat. Beat the egg with the sugar until light and creamy. Add the melted butter and mix in with a whisk, then add the crème fraîche or soured cream in two lots. | 2 | Mix the flour, salt and baking powder in a bowl. Remove the blueberries from the freezer and mix them with the flour. Make a well in the centre then tip in the liquid ingredients and stir rapidly. | ➢ |

3	Fill the moulds two-thirds full with the batter (work quickly so that the blueberries do not defrost) then tap the tins or tray on the work top to settle the mixture. Transfer to the oven and bake for 25 minutes (or for 15 minutes for smaller ones).

TIP
❈

☛ Make sure you do not overwork the mixture, which tends to make the muffins hard. Do not fill the moulds right to the top, so that the batter rises into a pleasing dome top.

 4 — Remove the muffins from the oven, run the blade of a knife around each one then leave to cool in the moulds for 10 minutes before turning out onto a wire rack.

TO SERVE
✳

Enjoy these muffins the American way, for breakfast, with a knob of butter and served with tea or coffee.

CHOCOLATE MUFFINS

VARIATION ON BLUEBERRY MUFFINS
❋

Sift 100g (3½ oz) flour, 25 g (1 oz) cocoa powder and ½ teaspoon baking powder.

In a second bowl, beat 75 g (3 oz) sugar with 2 eggs. Add 100 g (3½ oz) warm melted butter then

75 ml (3 fl oz) milk. Lightly mix into the flour, adding 50 g (2 oz) chopped chocolate at the end.

BANANA MUFFINS

VARIATION ON BLUEBERRY MUFFINS
❊

Mix together 135 g (4½ oz) flour, ½ teaspoon each of bicarbonate of soda, baking powder and cinnamon and a pinch of salt. In a second bowl, beat 150 g (5 oz) sugar with 1 egg. Add 40 g (1½ oz) warm melted butter, 2 small ripe mashed bananas and 25 ml (1 fl oz) milk. Lightly mix into the flour.

BRAN & RAISIN MUFFINS

VARIATION ON BLUEBERRY MUFFINS
❊

Soak 75 g (3 oz) All-Bran® in 230 ml (7½ fl oz) milk. In a large bowl, beat 100 g (3½ oz) golden granulated sugar with 1 egg, add 50 ml (2 fl oz) sunflower oil, then ¼ teaspoon vanilla extract. Add the All-Bran® and milk. In a second bowl, mix 125 g (4 oz) flour, ¼ teaspoon bicarbonate of soda and a pinch of salt. Lightly mix in the liquid ingredients, adding 75 g (3 oz) raisins at the end.

OAT & APPLE MUFFINS

VARIATION ON BLUEBERRY MUFFINS
❋

Soak 75 g (3 oz) porridge oats in 175 ml (6 fl oz) milk. Beat 50 g (2 oz) golden granulated sugar with 1 egg, pour in 50 g (2 oz) melted butter and ¼ teaspoon vanilla extract. In another bowl, mix together 100 g (3½ oz) flour, ¼ teaspoon baking powder and a pinch each of cinnamon and salt. Lightly mix in the liquid ingredients and incorporate 65 g (2½ oz) diced apple at the end.

MADELEINES

⇢ MAKES 18 • PREPARATION: 20 MINUTES • COOKING: 10 MINUTES • RESTING: AT LEAST 2 HOURS ⇠

2 whole eggs + 1 egg yolk
75 g (3 oz) butter
½ vanilla pod
75 g (3 oz) sugar

65 g (2½ oz) flour
½ teaspoon baking powder
½ teaspoon salt

IN ADVANCE:
Beat the eggs and the yolk together in a small bowl.

1	Melt the butter and keep warm over a low heat.	2	Add the seeds from the vanilla pod to the eggs with the sugar and whisk well.	3	Mix the flour with the baking powder and salt.
4	Sprinkle the flour over the egg mixture and mix with a flexible spatula until evenly blended.	5	Pour on the warm butter in a stream while continuing to mix with the spatula.	6	Cover the batter and rest in a cool place for at least 2 hours (and up to 12 hours).

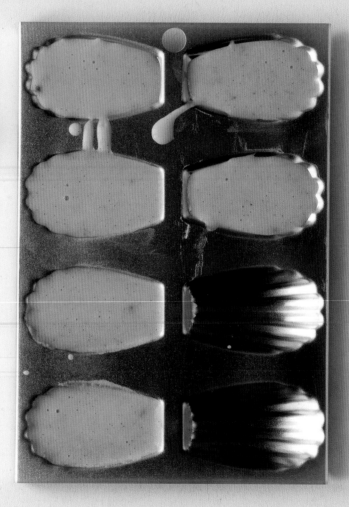

7

Preheat the oven to 210°C (400°F), Gas Mark 6. Carefully butter then flour an 8-hole madeleine tin. Shake the tin to remove the surplus. Spoon the batter into the moulds and fill almost level to the top.

TIPS
❋

When resting the batter it is best to cover with cling film placed directly on the surface. If you have nonstick moulds, there is no need to butter and flour them. Note: the oven must be very hot if the madeleines are to rise and cook before they dry out.

8	Transfer to the oven for about 10 minutes.

TURNING OUT
❈

Turn out the madeleines once they come out of the oven, then put them back in their moulds to cool. Allow them to become completely cold before eating.

TIP
❈

☛ After 2–3 minutes the rims of the madeleines should be a little risen. Reduce the oven temperature to 160°C (325°F), Gas Mark 3 and continue to cook for about 8 minutes, or until the madeleines are golden-brown.

CHOCOLATE MACAROONS

❖ **MAKES 10** • PREPARATION: 25 MINUTES • COOKING: 11 MINUTES • RESTING: AT LEAST 20 MINUTES ❖

FOR THE MACAROONS:
40 g (1½ oz) ground almonds
75 g (3 oz) icing sugar
10 g (½ oz) cocoa powder

1 egg white
10 g (½ oz) caster sugar
2 drops red food colouring
100 g (3½ oz) Chocolate Ganache
(see recipe 07)

IN ADVANCE:
Prepare a baking sheet covered with
silicone paper.

1 2
3 4

1	Whiz the ground almonds, icing sugar and cocoa powder in a food-processor until fine. Stop the motor frequently and stir with a spatula to prevent the mixture from sticking.	2	Sift this powder through a fine-mesh sieve.	
3	Whisk the egg whites. When they begin to hold their shape, gradually add the sugar and continue to whisk until the whites are firm.	4	Add the food colouring, drop by drop, and mix gently with a flexible spatula until the colour is uniform.	➤

5 6
7 8

5	Sprinkle the dry ingredients a little at a time on the meringue, incorporating each addition with the flexible spatula.	6	Work carefully. You want to end up with an evenly blended mixture.
7	Fill a piping bag and form small macaroons, well spaced on the prepared baking sheet. Tap the sheet on the work surface. Preheat the oven to 160°C (325°F), Gas Mark 3.	8	Leave the macaroons in the warmest part of the room to form a crust (it can take several hours if the air is damp). Press lightly on one macaroon to check that it no longer sticks.

9	Transfer the baking sheet to the oven and bake for 11 minutes for small macaroons, 15 minutes for medium ones.

TIP
❀

 Wait until the macaroons are cold before peeling them from the paper.

FILLING
❀

Put a knob of ganache in the centre of the flat side of a macaroon shell then press the flat side of a second macaroon onto the ganache. Press together until the ganache spreads out to the sides.

RASPBERRY MACAROONS

VARIATION ON CHOCOLATE MACAROONS
❋

Prepare the macaroons, following recipe 53, omitting the cocoa and tinting the egg whites with 6 drops of red food colouring. Instead of ganache, fill with 100 g (3½ oz) raspberry jam.

CARAMEL MACAROONS

VARIATION ON CHOCOLATE MACAROONS
❋

Prepare the macaroons, following recipe 53, but adding ½ teaspoon cocoa powder and tinting the egg whites with 1 drop of red food colouring and 1 drop of yellow. Instead of ganache, fill the macaroons with 100 g (3½ oz) salty butter caramel sauce (see recipe 10).

STAR BUNS

⇒ **MAKES 8** • PREPARATION: 20 MINUTES • COOKING: 1 HOUR 15 MINUTES • RESTING: 12 HOURS ⇐

1 vanilla pod
250 ml (8 fl oz) milk
125 g (4 oz) golden granulated sugar
50 g (2 oz) flour

1 whole egg + 1 egg yolk
25 g (1 oz) butter
2 teaspoons rum

IN ADVANCE:
Split the vanilla pod in two and scrape the seeds into the milk.

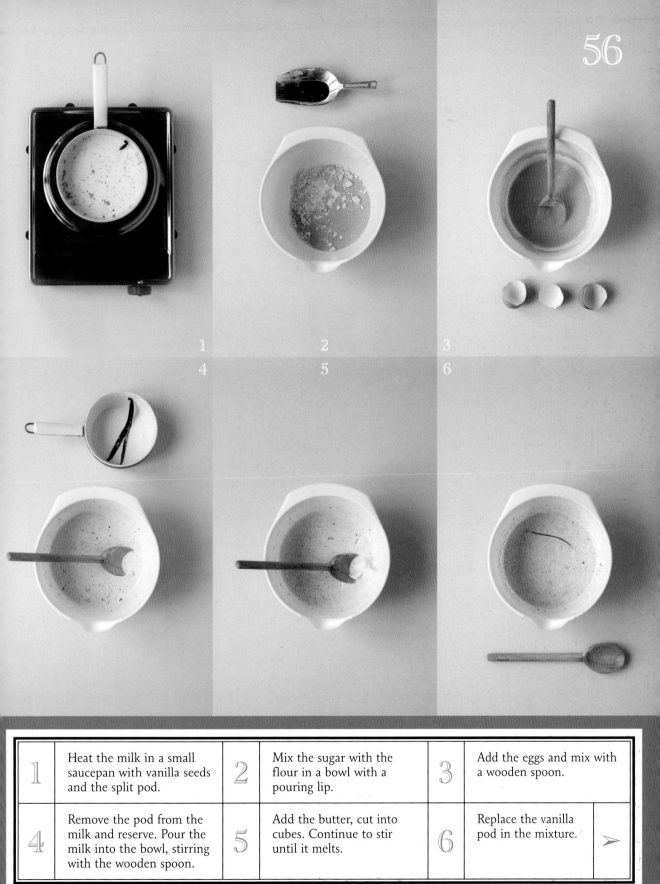

1	Heat the milk in a small saucepan with vanilla seeds and the split pod.	2	Mix the sugar with the flour in a bowl with a pouring lip.	3	Add the eggs and mix with a wooden spoon.
4	Remove the pod from the milk and reserve. Pour the milk into the bowl, stirring with the wooden spoon.	5	Add the butter, cut into cubes. Continue to stir until it melts.	6	Replace the vanilla pod in the mixture. ➤

7 8
9 10

7	Allow the mixture to cool to room temperature before adding the rum. Stir and cover with cling film. Refrigerate for at least 12 hours.	8	Take the batter from the fridge 1 hour before you want to cook. Preheat the oven to its highest setting and position a rack in the centre.
9	Whisk the batter until it is evenly blended again and remove the vanilla pod.	10	Place your moulds on a baking sheet and fill them three-quarters full or to within 1 cm (½ in) of the top. Transfer them to the oven.

11 Allow the batter to expand and colour (about 10 minutes). When the buns are nicely golden-brown, reduce the temperature to 180°C (350°F), Gas Mark 4. Continue to cook until the visible part is dark brown and feels firm when pressed with a finger (allow 60–70 minutes). Leave them to cool before turning them out of the moulds.

TIP
☞ For preference, use an 8-hole star-shaped silicone tray if you can find one, rather than a metal one. Alternatively, a small silicone muffin tray or individual moulds could be used.

5	Pour this mixture over the dry ingredients.	6	Beat with a wooden spoon until the mixture is evenly blended.
7	Add the remaining flour and mix again until it is fully incorporated.	8	Place the dough on a well-floured work surface and roll out using a floured rolling pin until the dough is about 1 cm (½ in) in thickness.

9

Use 2 floured dough cutters, one 9 cm (3½ in)
and the other 3 cm (1 in), to make rings. Place
them on a large plate. Gather up the trimmings
and work them quickly into a ball then flatten.
Roll out as before to make more doughnuts
until all the dough is used up.

TIP
☀

☞ The doughnut dough is very sticky,
which is why you need to liberally flour the
work surface, the rolling pin and the cutters
to ensure your rings are evenly shaped.

10 11
12 13

10	Carefully lower the doughnuts into the hot oil, as many as possible without them overlapping.	11	When they rise to the surface and are nicely golden (this takes about 2 minutes), turn them over using a slotted spoon.
12	Allow them to cook for 1 further minute.	13	Remove the doughnuts using the slotted spoon when they are golden on the second side.

14 Drain the doughnuts on a raised wire rack or on kitchen paper. Allow the oil to return to temperature before frying another batch. Meanwhile, turn the hot doughnuts in the cinnamon sugar.

TIP

☞ If you don't have a deep fryer, it is best to use a cast-iron pan which retains the heat well, so the oil will not cool too much between batches.

MAPLE SYRUP GLAZE

❖ ENOUGH FOR 12 DOUGHNUTS · PREPARATION: 5 MINUTES ❖

50 g (2 oz) icing sugar
40 ml (1½ fl oz) maple syrup

Sift the icing sugar into a small
bowl. Pour the maple syrup over
the icing sugar. Whisk vigorously.

GLAZING ❋	TIPS ❋
Trickle the glaze over the doughnuts and spread with a small spatula. Wait a few minutes for the glaze to set. You can also pour the glaze onto a plate and dip the doughnuts in one by one before allowing them to drain over the plate. Place them on a wire rack.	For a more runny glaze, add up to 10 ml (½ fl oz) extra maple syrup. Take care not to make fingerprints: this glaze does not set completely.

CHOCOLATE CHIP COOKIES

❖ MAKES 12 • PREPARATION: 25 MINUTES • RESTING: 10 MINUTES • COOKING: 14 MINUTES ❖

75 g (3 oz) butter
100 g (3½ oz) plain dark chocolate
(minimum 52% cocoa solids)
100 g (3½ oz) golden granulated sugar
50 g (2 oz) caster sugar

1 egg yolk at room temperature
½ teaspoon vanilla extract
125 g (4 oz) self-raising flour
½ teaspoon bicarbonate of soda
½ teaspoon salt

IN ADVANCE:
Preheat the oven to 170°C (340°F),
Gas Mark 3. Put a shelf in the centre of the
oven. Melt the butter in a small saucepan,
remove from the heat and allow to cool.

1 2
3 4

1	Cut up the chocolate into chip-size pieces (about 4 from each square).	2	In a large bowl, mix the golden granulated sugar and the caster sugar.	
3	Add the warm melted butter and beat with an electric whisk until mixed thoroughly.	4	Add the egg and the vanilla extract. Beat again to incorporate.	➤

5 6
7 8

5	Mix together the flour, bicarbonate and salt. Add to the liquid ingredients and beat on slow speed, just enough to incorporate the flour.	6	Add the chocolate chips and mix with a flexible spatula to distribute them in the mixture.
7	Cover the mixture with cling film and refrigerate for 10 minutes. Meanwhile, cover a baking sheet with baking paper.	8	Remove the mixture from the fridge and form into large balls. Use both hands to divide the balls into two with a quick twist. Place them on the baking sheet, uneven side uppermost.

9   Make sure the cookies are well spaced so that they can spread out during cooking. Transfer to the oven and cook for no longer than 14 minutes. Allow the cookies to cool on the baking sheet placed on a wire rack before removing them using a long thin spatula.

HANDY HINTS

On no account try to remove the cookies from the paper as soon as they come out of the oven; you need to wait at least 15 minutes. These cookies stay very soft, even when completely cold. For cookies thicker than shown in the photograph, the melted butter needs to be completely cooled before it is mixed with the sugars (step 3).

ALMOST OREOS®

❧ **MAKES 20** • PREPARATION: 25 MINUTES • RESTING: 1 HOUR 45 MINUTES + 30 MINUTES • COOKING: 2 x 12 MINUTES ❧

140 g (4½ oz) plain flour
½ teaspoon salt
1 tablespoon cocoa powder
75 g (3 oz) caster sugar
25 g (1 oz) icing sugar
25 g (1 oz) plain dark chocolate

100 g (3½ oz) softened butter
1 egg yolk at room temperature
½ teaspoon vanilla extract
GANACHE:
125 g (4 oz) white chocolate
40 ml (1½ fl oz) crème fraîche

IN ADVANCE:
Mix together the flour, salt and sifted cocoa powder in a bowl. Mix together the sugar and icing sugar in a separate bowl. Melt the dark chocolate over a very gentle heat.

1 2
3 4

1	Beat the softened butter in a large bowl, using an electric whisk. Add the sugars and beat again for 1 minute until the mixture is light and fluffy.	2	Scrape the sides of the bowl with a flexible spatula. Add the egg yolk, vanilla extract and melted chocolate. Beat well to incorporate all the ingredients.
3	Scrape the sides of the bowl again, then add in the dry ingredients.	4	Mix on slow speed, until a dough forms.

5 6
7 8

5	Place the dough on a clean work surface and shape it into a cylinder approximately 15 cm (6 in) long.	6	Roll the cylinder on the work surface to even it out.
7	Wrap the dough in cling film and refrigerate for at least 1 hour 30 minutes. Preheat the oven to 160°C (325°F), Gas Mark 3. Cover 2 baking sheets with baking paper.	8	Remove the dough from the fridge and place on a board. Using a sharp knife, trim off the ends then slice the cylinder into 40 very thin rounds (2.5 mm/⅛ in).

9	Place the rounds on the 2 baking sheets and cook them in 2 batches, each for 12 minutes.

COOKING HINT
❊

Cut 20 rounds of the dough and put them on a baking sheet to cook immediately. You can slice the remainder while the first batch is cooling on the baking sheet.

TIPS
❊

☛ If your kitchen is quite warm, cut the cylinder of dough in half and refrigerate one half while you slice the other. It's worth turning the cylinder at regular intervals so that it doesn't flatten on one side under its own weight. You can keep the wrapped dough for up to 3 days in the fridge before cooking.

➤

10 11
12 13

10	To make the ganache, first melt the white chocolate over a very gentle heat or in a bain-marie.	11	Add the crème fraîche, mix together and allow to cool for approximately 15 minutes at room temperature.
12	Turn half the cookies upside down on a baking sheet and put a teaspoonful of ganache in the centre of each.	13	Top with the remaining cookies and press gently together so that the ganache spreads until you can see it round the sides.

14	Put the assembled cookies in the fridge in a sealed container. Leave them for at least 30 minutes before eating to allow the ganache to set. They will keep for several days stored in this way.

VARIATION

※

Replace the white chocolate with plain dark chocolate and the crème fraîche with whipping cream. Begin by simmering the cream before adding the chocolate, off the heat. Mix together then allow to cool to room temperature before use.

SCONES

❖ MAKES 10 • PREPARATION: 20 MINUTES • COOKING: 14 MINUTES ❖

275 g (9 oz) plain flour + extra for
rolling out
3 teaspoons baking powder
large pinch of salt
65 g (2½ oz) cold butter

50 g (2 oz) raisins, chopped
1 egg
40 g (1½ oz) sugar
150ml (¼ pint) single or whipping cream
+ extra for glazing

IN ADVANCE:
Preheat the oven to 220°C (425°F), Gas
Mark 7. Cover a baking sheet with baking
paper. Have ready a little flour in a bowl
and a little cream for glazing in another.

1	Mix the flour, baking powder and salt in a large bowl. Dice the butter and rub it into the dry ingredients until the mixture forms crumbs.	2	Add the chopped raisins and mix to incorporate. Make a well in the centre.	
3	Whisk together the egg and the sugar in a bowl until the mixture is light and creamy. Add the pouring cream and mix again.	4	Pour this mixture into the well. Mix with a flexible spatula until a dough forms.	➤

7 Flour the work surface and tip the dough on top. Quickly work the dough until it is even and smooth. Flatten to form a slab about 3–4 cm (at least 1–1¾ in) thick. Flour the top and even out with the rolling pin. Dip a 5-cm (2-in) round cutter in the prepared bowl of flour. Cut out as many scones as possible, flouring the cutter between each one.

TIP

Try to avoid pushing the scones out from the cutter; instead, let them drop onto the baking sheet from the cutter by shaking it from the bottom.

| 8 | Glaze the tops of the scones with a little cream. Transfer to the oven and cook for 14 minutes. Remove immediately to cool on a wire rack. | **SCONES AND STRAWBERRY BUTTER**
❊
For 20 scones: 100 g (3½ oz) softened butter, 75 g (3 oz) strawberry jam at room temperature. Whisk the soft butter until it becomes pale. Incorporate the jam and whisk again until it is evenly blended (but not too much; ideally, little specks of jam should remain visible). Serve with the warm scones. |

PECAN BISCUITS

✈ MAKES 10 • PREPARATION: 20 MINUTES • COOKING: 20 MINUTES ✦

125 g (4 oz) flour
½ teaspoon salt
50 g (2 oz) pecan nuts, chopped
100 g (3½ oz) softened butter

25 g (1 oz) sugar
¼ teaspoon vanilla extract
icing sugar, for dusting

IN ADVANCE:
Preheat the oven to 170°C (340°F), Gas Mark 3. Cover a baking sheet with baking paper. Mix the flour, salt and nuts.

1 2
3 4

1	Beat the softened butter with the sugar. Add the vanilla then beat in the flour mixture.	2	Work with a flexible spatula until you have a smooth dough.
3	Divide into 10 pieces and shape them into balls the size of a ping-pong ball.	4	Place on the baking sheet. Transfer to the oven and cook for 20 minutes. Allow to cool on the sheet. Dust with icing sugar just before serving.

BRETON BISCUITS

➤ **MAKES 20** • PREPARATION: 30 MINUTES • RESTING: 30 MINUTES • COOKING: 14 MINUTES ⬥

100 g (3½ oz) golden granulated sugar
100 g (3½ oz) best-quality salted butter
1 egg yolk at room temperature
125 g (4 oz) plain flour

IN ADVANCE:
Whiz the sugar in a food processor for
2–3 minutes to make it finer.

Preheat the oven to 180°C (350°F),
Gas Mark 4 after the dough has rested.

1	Work the butter in a bowl using a wooden spatula until it forms a pomade.	2	Add the sugar and beat with an electric whisk, slowly at first, and gradually increasing the speed.
3	Continue to beat until the mixture is creamy (but not for too long, otherwise the butter will warm up).	4	Add the egg yolk and mix with a whisk just enough to incorporate. ➤

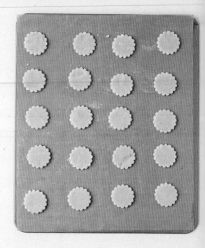

5	Tip in the flour and mix again with the whisk until a dough forms.	6	Quickly work the dough with the palm of your hand until smooth.	7	Shape into a flattened ball and wrap it in cling film. Refrigerate for 30 minutes.
8	Remove the dough and place on a lightly floured work surface. Roll out to a thickness of 5 mm (¼ in).	9	Using a 5-cm (2-in) fluted cutter, cut out the biscuits.	10	Place the biscuits on a sheet covered with baking paper. Transfer to the oven and cook for 14 minutes.

	The biscuits should be lightly coloured. Remove them from the oven and leave on the baking sheet on a wire rack.	**STORAGE** ❊
11		Store these biscuits at room temperature in a tin (not a completely sealed container so that their moisture can escape). How long they will keep depends on the humidity level of the room.

BLUEBERRY PANCAKES

✈ **MAKES 16** • **PREPARATION: 15 MINUTES** • **COOKING: 5 MINUTES** ✦

65 g (2½ oz) butter
450 ml (¾ pint) milk at room temperature
2 teaspoons lemon juice
1 egg at room temperature
275 g (9 oz) flour
3 teaspoons or 1 sachet baking powder

1 teaspoon bicarbonate of soda
25 g (1 oz) caster sugar
1 teaspoon salt
125 g (4 oz) frozen blueberries (weigh then keep them frozen)
maple syrup

IN ADVANCE:

Melt the butter in a low-sided frying pan. Leave a thin film in the pan for cooking the pancakes and pour off the rest and reserve it for the batter. Keep the frying pan over a low heat while you make the batter.

1	Mix together the milk and the lemon juice.	2	Break the egg into the milk and whisk.	3	Add the reserved melted butter and whisk again.
4	Sift together the flour, baking powder, bicarbonate of soda, sugar and salt in a large bowl.	5	Make a well in the centre. Pour in the liquid ingredients and beat with a hand whisk.	6	Stop as soon as the batter is smooth (overbeating makes the pancakes dry).

7 8
9 10

7	Increase the heat under the frying pan to medium. Pour in separate ladlefuls of batter; do not allow the pancakes to touch as they spread.	8	Remove the blueberries from the freezer and sprinkle generously over the pancakes.
9	Cook until bubbles appear on the surface and the underside is a good pale-brown colour (2 minutes at the most).	10	Flip over the pancakes and cook until the second side is also a good colour.

11	Remove the pancakes from the frying pan and keep warm in the oven at 100°C (220°F), Gas Mark ¼. Prepare the remainder in batches until all the batter is used up.

TO SERVE
❈

Stack the pancakes on serving plates and drizzle with maple syrup.

TIP
❈

☛ Ideally, have several non-stick frying pans heating at the same time so that you can cook all the pancakes in one go. If, however, you are working with a single frying pan, dip some kitchen paper in the melted butter prepared for the batter and keep handy in a bowl: use this to oil the pan each time you cook a batch.

TARTS

5

Sweet shortcrust pastry 66
Tarte tatin 67
Custard tart 68
Lemon meringue pie 69
Kiwi & mascarpone tartlets 70
Strawberry tartlets 71

SWEET SHORTCRUST PASTRY

❧ **MAKES 400 G (13 OZ)** • PREPARATION: 15 MINUTES • RESTING: 30 MINUTES ❧

100 g (3½ oz) butter
200 g (7 oz) plain flour + extra for dusting
20 ml (¾ fl oz) water

20 g (¾ oz) sugar
½ teaspoon salt
1 egg

IN ADVANCE:
Cut the butter into cubes and place on the flour on your work surface.

1 2
3 4

1	Rub the butter into the flour until the mixture resembles breadcrumbs. Make a well in the centre. Pour in the water, sugar, salt and the egg.	2	Dissolve the sugar and salt using your fingertips. Work the flour mixture into the liquid in the centre; the dough will be fairly wet.
3	Bring in all the remaining flour and squeeze it with both hands. Form a ball but don't over-knead it. Flatten into a slab 3–4 cm (1–1¾ in) thick and wrap in cling film.	4	Refrigerate the dough for at least 30 minutes (flattening the dough speeds up the chilling time) before rolling it out with a rolling pin.

TARTE TATIN

❧ SERVES 6–8 • PREPARATION: 25 MINUTES • COOKING: 1 HOUR 20 MINUTES ❧

65 ml (2½ fl oz) water
200 g (7 oz) sugar
65 g (2½ oz) salted butter

1 kg (2 lb) tart green apples
200 g (7 oz) Sweet Shortcrust Pastry
(see recipe 66)

IN ADVANCE:
Preheat the oven to 220°C (425°F),
Gas Mark 7 and put a shelf in the centre
of the oven.

1 2
3 4

1	Put the water then the sugar into a saucepan. Whisk over a medium heat to dissolve the sugar (see recipe 09).	2	Bring to the boil. As soon as it boils, stop stirring immediately and leave the caramel to colour until it turns amber.	
3	Remove from the heat and add the butter in pieces. Mix with the whisk until the butter is incorporated.	4	Pour the caramel into the base of a 24-cm (9½-in) solid-based cake tin.	➤

5 6
7 8

5	Peel and core the apples. Cut into quarters.	6	Tightly pack the quarters into the tin, with the peeled side up. Arrange the remaining quarters on top, filling in the gaps.
7	Transfer to the oven and bake for 1 hour. Remove the pastry from the fridge 15 minutes before the end of the cooking time.	8	Roll out the pastry to a round 24 cm (9½ in) in diameter. Place on top of the apples and bake the tart for a further 15–20 minutes.

9	Remove the tart from the oven. Immediately invert it onto a serving plate. Allow to cool slightly before serving.

OPTION
❈

Serve the tart warm with Chantilly cream (see recipe 14) or crème fraîche.

HANDY HINT
❈

The caramel may crystallize (as shown in the photo for step 4) when you add the butter, but it will melt again in the oven. To prevent it crystallizing, add ½ teaspoon of lemon juice to the sugar–water mix.

CUSTARD TART

❖ **SERVES 8** • PREPARATION: 25 MINUTES • COOKING: 50 MINUTES ❖

butter and a little flour, for preparing the
baking dish
300 g (10 oz) Sweet Shortcrust Pastry
(see recipe 66)
1 egg, for glazing

FOR THE CUSTARD:
1 litre (1¼ pints) milk
220 g (7½ oz) sugar
2 whole eggs + 1 egg yolk
125 g (4 oz) cornflour

1 teaspoon vanilla extract + ½ teaspoon salt
IN ADVANCE:
Preheat the oven to 200°C (400°F), Gas
Mark 6. Grease and flour a square baking
dish then lightly tap out the excess flour.

1	Roll out the pastry to a thickness of about 3 mm (⅛ in) and place it in the dish; it should overlap the sides a little.	2	Pinch up the edges of the pastry to make a rim (to stop it shrinking during cooking). Run the rolling pin over the top to trim off the overlap.	
3	Prick the pastry base with a fork then line the base and sides with lightly buttered baking paper. Blind bake for 10 minutes. Remove the paper.	4	Glaze the pastry with beaten egg then return to the oven for 3–4 minutes to dry. Remove the dish and turn up the heat to 220°C (425°F), Gas Mark 7.	➤

5 6
7 8

5	Pour 750 ml (1¼ pints) of the milk into a saucepan. Add the sugar, stir, and bring to the boil. Beat the eggs and egg yolk in a bowl.	6	Pour the rest of milk into another bowl, add the cornflour and whisk immediately. Stir in the beaten eggs, the vanilla and the salt.
7	Strain the mixture through a fine-mesh sieve to filter out the bits of yolk casing (which would otherwise coagulate during cooking).	8	When the milk reaches boiling point, remove the pan from the heat. Slowly pour on the egg mixture, whisking well. The cream will thicken.

| 9 | Pour the custard into the tart case and transfer to the oven for 35 minutes. Remove the tart and place on a wire rack to cool. Wrap in cling film and refrigerate to chill completely before serving. | **VARIATIONS**
❈
When you are short of time, you can make the custard without its pastry base. You can also use a sachet of vanilla sugar in place of the vanilla extract, in which case reduce the amount of caster sugar by 15 g (½ oz). |

LEMON MERINGUE PIE

❧ **SERVES 8** • PREPARATION: 30 MINUTES • COOKING: 25 MINUTES • RESTING: 15 MINUTES ❧

400 g (13 oz) Sweet Shortcrust Pastry
(see recipe 66)
350 g (12 oz) Confectioner's Cream (see
recipe 02), see step 5
½ vanilla pod, split in two

juice and rind of ½ lemon, unwaxed
2 egg whites
125 g (4 oz) caster sugar
2 tablespoons water
15 g (½ oz) icing sugar

IN ADVANCE:
Grease a 28-cm (11-in) tart tin and place
in the fridge.

1 2
3 4

1	Roll out the pastry in a round a little larger than the diameter of your tin. Prick it all over using a fork.	2	Carefully pick up the pastry and turn it over on the tin so that the pricked side is face down. Line the tin with the pastry, pressing it firmly against the sides.	
3	Run a rolling pin over the top to trim off the overlap. Refrigerate for 15 minutes. Preheat the oven to 170°C (340°F), Gas Mark 3.	4	Fill the pastry with baking beans and bake blind for 20 minutes then for 10 minutes without beans. Allow to cool.	➤

| 5 | Prepare the confectioner's cream (see recipe 02) by bringing the milk to the boil with the split vanilla pod and its scraped-out seeds. | Add the lemon juice and rind at the end of cooking. Cover with cling film placed directly on the surface and leave to become cold. |

6
7 8

	TO MAKE ITALIAN MERINGUE			
6	Whisk the egg whites until stiff, adding a teaspoonful of caster sugar halfway through.	8	Boil to the 'ball' stage, which takes about 3 minutes. Pour the boiling syrup over the egg whites, allowing it to run in a stream between the whisk and the sides of the bowl. Whisk for about 5 minutes on a slow speed to cool the mixture.	➤
7	Mix the remaining sugar with the water in a saucepan and bring to the boil.			

| 9 | Incorporate one-third of the meringue in the confectioner's cream to lighten its texture. Preheat the grill. | 10 | Cover the base of the cooled pastry case with the confectioner's cream. Top this with meringue, making little peaks all over the surface. |

| 11 | Sprinkle with icing sugar and flash the tart under the hot grill (up to 2 minutes) to brown the meringue lightly. | **TIP**
❋
To make peaks on the meringue, lightly strike the surface using the back of a small spoon. |

KIWI & MASCARPONE TARTLETS

➤ **MAKES 6 • PREPARATION: 30 MINUTES** ◀

TART BASE:
100 g (3½ oz) plain biscuits
65 g (2½ oz) butter
25 g (1 oz) caster sugar

MASCARPONE FILLING:
175 g (6 oz) mascarpone
30 g (1¼ oz) icing sugar
½ sachet (½ teaspoon) vanilla sugar

4 kiwi fruit

		OPTION ❋	
1	Whiz the biscuits in a food processor for 30–60 seconds to reduce them to crumbs.	You can also crush the biscuits by putting them in a clean tea towel and running a rolling pin over the top.	
		TIP ❋	
		☞ If any large lumps remain, crush them between your fingers.	

2 3
4 5

2	Melt the butter in a saucepan. Mix together the sugar and the crushed biscuits in a bowl, then pour the butter on top.	3	Mix with a fork until the crumbs resemble wet sand.
4	Divide the biscuit crumbs between 6 tartlet tins. Even them out with the back of a spoon and press down with a flat-based object. Smooth the base and sides with the back of the spoon.	5	Put the tartlet tins into the fridge to firm up the bases (the butter will solidify). Meanwhile use a fork to beat together the mascarpone, icing sugar and vanilla sugar.

		NOTE
		❋
6	Spread the mascarpone over the tartlet bases. Peel the kiwi fruit and cut them into slices about 8 mm (⅓ in) thick. Arrange them, overlapping slightly, on top of the cream. Cover with cling film and refrigerate until ready to serve.	Do not leave the tartlets in the fridge for longer than 2 hours, otherwise the bases will become soggy.

STRAWBERRY TARTLETS

❖ MAKES 6 • PREPARATION: 30 MINUTES • COOKING: 10 MINUTES • RESTING: 10 MINUTES ❖

200 g (7 oz) Sweet Shortcrust Pastry
(see recipe 66)
150 g (5 oz) Almond Cream (see recipe 04)
600 g (1 lb 5 oz) small strawberries

IN ADVANCE:
Preheat the oven to 220°C (425°F),
Gas Mark 7.

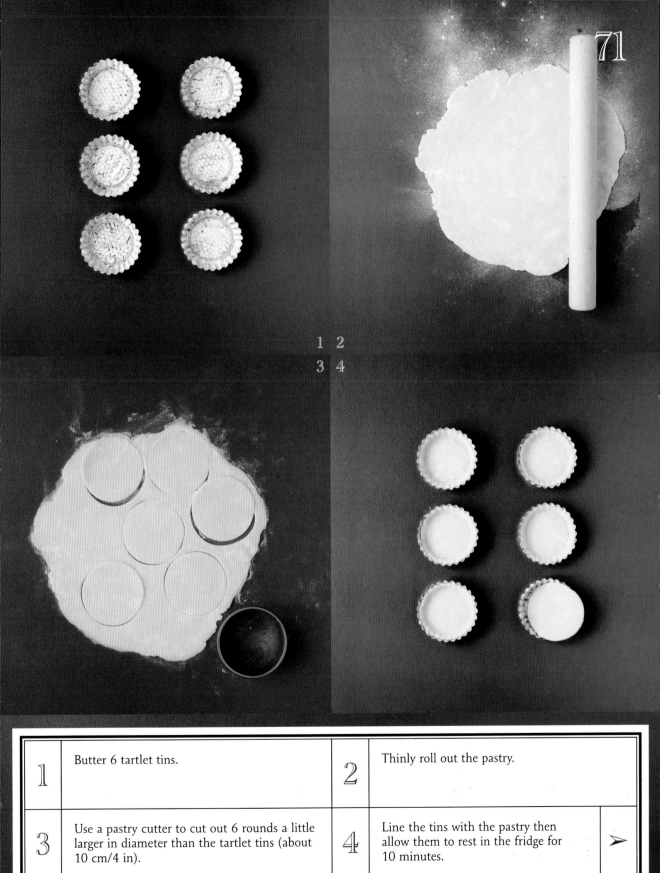

1	Butter 6 tartlet tins.	2	Thinly roll out the pastry.
3	Use a pastry cutter to cut out 6 rounds a little larger in diameter than the tartlet tins (about 10 cm/4 in).	4	Line the tins with the pastry then allow them to rest in the fridge for 10 minutes. ➤

5 6
7 8

5	Spread the cream over each tartlet shell and smooth it with the back of a spoon. Transfer to the oven and cook for 10 minutes.	6	Meanwhile, rinse and dry the strawberries on kitchen paper. Hull them by trimming off the base.
7	Remove the tartlets from the oven and place on a wire rack to cool.	8	When the tartlets are completely cold, decorate with strawberries.

TIP	OPTION
☞ Choose strawberries that are roughly the same size. Don't use really large ones as they are more difficult to cut with a pastry fork.	You can also thinly slice the strawberries and arrange them, slightly overlapping, in rose fashion. This way, you will use fewer berries.

APPENDICES

GLOSSARY

TABLE OF CONTENTS

INDEX OF RECIPES

GENERAL INDEX

ACKNOWLEDGEMENTS

GLOSSARY

BAIN-MARIE (WATER BATH)

Using a bain-marie or water bath is a method of cooking that allows a dish to be heated more gently than is possible by exposing it directly to the heat source. This gentle cooking is achieved by placing the cake tin or mould inside another, larger, tin that contains boiling water.

Cooking with a bain-marie also prevents a dish from drying out. Once in the hot oven, the evaporating water continuously produces vapour and keeps the heat moist. For this purpose, there is no need to sit the dish directly in the water bath: you can put a shallow tray or tin under the shelf on which you intend to cook your dish. The water bath should be placed in the oven when you preheat it. Then, when you are ready to cook, pour in the equivalent of a small saucepan of very hot water into the shallow tray.

Using a bain-marie is also a good way to defrost frozen fruit. Place the fruit in a bowl and cover with cling film. Put the bowl over a saucepan of boiling water and leave for the required time (about 10 minutes for red fruit), stirring mid-way through. Defrosting by this method means that the fruits retain their colour and their juice as they defrost.

Sometimes a recipe calls for ingredients to be chilled very quickly as, for example, when making Chantilly cream (recipe 14). A cold-water bain-marie is made by filling a bowl larger than your mixing bowl with ice cubes and very cold water. The mixing bowl is then plunged into this bath to chill the contents.

BALL STAGE

The 'ball' describes a stage in cooking sugar. When white sugar is heated its water content evaporates. The temperature of the sugar rises and by degrees it transforms into caramel.

All the stages of this transformation have their technical names recognized and understood by professionals, but only the 'ball' stage is used in this book. In effect, the advanced stages of cooking sugar can be recognized by their colour: a caramel which is lighter or darker in tone. In contrast, the early stages of cooking sugar show no colour; to measure the temperature, either use a sugar thermometer or remove a little of the syrup with a spoon and drop it into a bowl of very cold water. If it forms a ball, it has reached the right temperature for making Italian meringue or a butter cream, for example. If the ball feels soft between your fingers, the syrup is less hot than if the ball feels hard. Ideally, you want a hard ball to form but since the sugar goes from one stage to the next very quickly it is better to use the sugar as soon as you see the ball form to avoid the risk of overcooking the sugar, which is then extremely difficult to work.

BLIND BAKE

This term refers to the partial or complete baking of a pastry case before it is filled. This pre-cooking stage prevents the pastry from being softened by its filling or by fruits that are added subsequently.

BOIL/SIMMER

A dish is 'boiling' when it is placed over a high heat and large bubbles appear on the surface. This represents a higher temperature than when it is 'simmering', which is when only small bubbles form on the surface.

BUTTER

Unless stated otherwise, the butter used in these recipes is unsalted.

CARAMEL

Caramel is what is produced when white sugar is cooked beyond the stages where it is no longer a syrup. To make this safely you must use a saucepan with a heavy base, because the pan needs to be able to withstand the very high temperatures needed for making caramel, and because a thick base will also ensure the heat diffuses more evenly. Pour in the water first, then the sugar. Never use more than one-third the weight of water to the weight of sugar (so, for 75 g/3 oz of sugar use no more than 25 ml/1 fl oz of water). Place over a steady medium heat. Dissolve the sugar using a hand whisk, taking care not to flick the mixture up the sides of the pan. Bring to the boil when the sugar has dissolved, never before (because if the sugar is still solid when it boils it will not subsequently dissolve). Leave the syrup to concentrate without touching the pan. Beyond 150°C (300°F) it will change to a caramel; it will start to take on colour.

To stop the cooking, you must remove the pan from the heat a few seconds before the required colour is achieved (the caramel will continue to colour off the heat), or plunge the base of the pan into cold water for a few seconds. This second method is less preferable because the caramel cools and hence thickens, rendering it less workable than a liquid caramel.

CLING FILM

Cling film, or cellophane, is an indispensable item in cake-baking (along with the flexible spatula and a set of electronic scales). It forms a barrier between the prepared dish and the air, one that protects it from oxidation and its consequences: drying out (hence a crust or skin), colour change, microbial contamination…

Some professionals 'contact seal' all their prepared dishes, meaning that the cling film is placed directly on the surface of the dish. In this book, this technique is above all recommended for the Confectioner's Cream (recipe 02), which tends to form a skin at the end of cooking. In most other cases, it is enough to stretch cling film over the bowl in which the dish is prepared.

COAGULATE, COAGULATION

Coagulation occurs when certain components of some liquid ingredients bind together to form a denser mass.

In baking, this can sometimes occur when heating eggs, which is why they should be cooked very gently. It rarely produces a required effect because coagulation of one ingredient (eggs, for example) is not desirable in the final dish (for instance an egg custard); it will be grainy and unevenly blended.

COAT, COATING

A coating is when a liquid achieves a consistency (mostly as a result of heating) sufficiently thick to coat the surface of an object that has been dipped in it. A spoon, for example, is no longer visible through the coating and is evenly covered by it. When cooking is involved, as in making custard or lemon curd, the coating has reached the desired thickness when you can draw a line through the coating on the back of a spoon and the line remains visible.

COLOUR, COLOURATION

This stage in cooking shows the change from the initial colour of a dish to another under the effect of heat. Colouration occurs as soon as the initial colour changes to another; it can go from a very light golden to a very dark brown.

CRUMBS (RUBBING-IN METHOD)

'Crumbs' are made by rubbing small pieces of butter into flour with your fingertips. This action means every grain of flour becomes coated in butter so that, little by little, you produce a pale coloured mixture in which only tiny pieces of butter remain. To prevent the butter becoming warm, this rubbing in is done above the flour and butter in the bowl; by lifting and letting the crumbs fall you are introducing air and so cooling the mix.

You can also make the crumbs in a food processor fitted with a blade. Put the flour and the cold cubed butter into the bowl and pulse for a few seconds. Next add the egg–water mixture in which the salt and sugar have been dissolved. Pulse the food processor again, just until the dough forms. Turn out onto the work surface and knead a little with your palm then finish the preparation following the recipe.

EGGS

All these recipes use large eggs that weigh approximately 70 g (3 oz) in the shell or 60 g (2½ oz) without the shell.

In cases where it may be necessary to halve the quantity of ingredients, you might need to divide a single egg in two. This is much easier if you break the egg, beat it, then use half only. For real precision, you can weigh the beaten egg using electronic scales: half a large egg will weigh 30 g (just over 1 oz).

Contrary to received wisdom, you should not whisk egg whites until they are really firm if you need to combine them with other ingredients. In effect, stiffly whisked meringue tends to form lumps which are difficult to incorporate, and the extra mixing that stirring them in implies has the effect of causing the meringue to collapse. It is therefore much better, especially for making chocolate mousse, to whisk egg whites until they are just supple, not firm. Then, work the whites in using a flexible spatula. This gentle action 'relaxes' the whites and breaks down any lumps that may be present.

ELECTRONIC SCALES

A set of electronic scales is an indispensable tool for baking (along with a flexible spatula and cling film) because it enables you to measure the smallest quantities (as well as large ones, naturally). Even a few extra grams of salt or baking powder can be all too apparent in the taste and the texture of the final product. See also Measuring.

FLEXIBLE SPATULA

A 'maryse' is the term used by French chefs to designate a flexible spatula made from rubber, plastic or silicone. This utensil is one of the indispensable trio (with the electronic scales and cling film) used in baking. It allows you to scrape the bowl perfectly clean, for example when you need to empty the contents of one to combine with the contents of another. In baking terms, every gram of a measured ingredient is important (see under Electronic scales) and, by using this type of spatula, you don't leave any on the sides of the bowl. The flexibility of the spatula also allows you to delicately combine most preparations, especially those that include whisked egg whites (see Eggs) or flour (see Mixture). No other baking utensil performs this task so ably.

FLOUR, FLOURING
When you roll out pastry, you need to regularly flour the work surface to prevent the pastry from sticking, while avoiding too much flour being incorporated in the dough. To effect this, scatter several pinches of flour on the work surface.

FLOUR TYPES
In baking terms, plain flour is generally reserved for bread-style cakes (banana bread, pancakes, gingerbread, and so forth) where the final result has a crust enclosing soft interior. Baking powder and/or bicarbonate of soda is sifted in with the plain flour. Self-raising flour is used for lighter cakes. It is worth seeking out the varieties sold as 'supersifted' or 'superfine', which are already sifted to ensure the grains are as fine and even as possible.

HOMOGENEOUS
A preparation is 'homogeneous' when its texture is even. That does not necessarily mean smooth: a homogeneous texture can be grainy, but it must be uniformly grainy. When a smooth texture is required, this is specified in the recipe.

MEASURES
A set of electronic scales is a real asset when cake-making, for accurately measuring your ingredients. However, most electronic scales are not calibrated to weigh liquids (measured in either millilitres or fluid ounces). It is useful, therefore, to know that 1 litre (1,000 ml) of water weighs 1 kilogram (1,000 g). Thus 15 g = 15 ml. Be careful though: this handy equivalent does not convert exactly for all liquids; oil in particular weighs a little less than water whereas milk weighs a little more. However, for most purposes, the differences are so slight that the approximation of 1 g = 1 ml can be followed whatever the liquid. In most recipes, the liquid ingredients have less effect on the chemistry of baking than the dry ingredients.

MIXTURE, MIXING
Most baking recipes use the following basic method: the dry ingredients are mixed together in one bowl, the liquid ingredients combined in another, then the two are brought together.

The mixing of dry ingredients rarely poses any problem (provided that the ingredients are correctly measured and the flour sifted); you can even prepare this stage in advance and keep the dry mixture for a day or two in a plastic bag or sealed box.

The mixing of liquids, however, can become a more delicate undertaking since the ingredients often have different temperatures (for example, melted butter that is still hot, eggs or milk taken directly from the fridge) or the temperature of one ingredient can affect another (melted butter will set if it is poured into cold milk), and this works against achieving a good mix. It is therefore important that the overall temperature of liquid ingredients is the same before they are combined.

• To warm up an egg, plunge it for 1–2 minutes in a bowl filled with hot water.

• To warm up milk, put it in a saucepan over a gentle heat.

• To cool melted butter, pour it into a cold bowl.

Mixing the dry and wet ingredients represents another delicate stage. It is at this point that baking powder is activated, but its raising action does not last very long. Once dry and liquid ingredients are combined, the dish must be transferred to the oven. Furthermore, when flour comes into contact with a liquid and is worked with a utensil, the all-important 'web' of gluten develops which is essential to the structure of a dough or batter. On the other hand, if this gluten network is overdeveloped, the cake can be transformed into a stone. For this reason it is often specified that you do not use an electric whisk to mix wet and dry ingredients; instead the recommendation is to work gently and as little as possible using a flexible spatula.

PIPING BAG, PIPING

A cone-shaped washable bag, usually with a set of nozzles of different sizes and shapes, is invaluable for making attractive individual buns or meringues on a baking sheet. It is also used for filling choux buns or for decorating the top of cakes with cream.

To fill the bag, start by sliding the nozzle into the base of the bag then block the nozzle by pushing a fold of the bag inside it. If you are right-handed, hold the bag in your left hand and fold back the top of the bag over your hand. Fill the bag with your free hand. Close the bag by turning it the other way up (nozzle pointing up) and twisting the end of the bag until the mixture starts to appear out of the nozzle. Squeeze to make the mixture ooze out and keep twisting the bag so that it is always tight.

POMADE

In baking terms, a pomade is the term for butter which is supple in texture but still remains a little firm. This texture makes it easier to blend with other ingredients without it losing its structure (unlike melted butter), and also to beat it until light and fluffy.

There are two ways of achieving a pomade. Start by cutting the butter into small pieces so that it warms up more quickly and uniformly.

Method one: Leave the butter at room temperature until you can push your finger into it easily; this can take anything from 20 minutes to several hours depending on the temperature of the room.

Method two: Put the chopped butter in a heat-resistant bowl and place over a saucepan of boiling water just removed from the heat. Leave the bowl above the heat source for a few seconds then remove and work the butter with a spatula until it forms a 'pomade'. If it proves hard work, place over the pan for a few more seconds.

ROLL OUT, ROLLING

This refers to pastry being rolled out using a rolling pin on a floured surface to the required size and thickness. The task of rolling out pastry evenly is easier if it is lifted and turned between each pass with the rolling pin. To ensure that the pastry doesn't stick to the work surface it should be lightly floured (see Flouring). You can also turn the pastry over at regular intervals and even up the edges with your fingers to achieve the required shape.

To divide a block in two, you need to roll the pastry out as a rectangle thin enough to be folded over then cut it with a sharp knife at the point of the fold.

To correctly position a circular pastry sheet in the tin, fold it in on itself twice to form a fan shape then place the point of the triangle on the centre of the tin. Unfold the sheet again and line the tin with the pastry, pressing it well into the angles and sides.

SIFT, SIFTING

Sifting flour removes any lumps by passing it through a strainer or fine sieve. You are strongly advised to sift your flour through a fine-mesh sieve for most if not all of these recipes, and it is well worth buying superfine flour, which is already sifted.

SIPHON

A siphon is an aluminium bottle that contains pressurized liquid gas. By activating the pump that controls the flow of the liquid up through a tube, the liquid is carbonated and so comes out in the form of mousse. This device allows you to transform sweetened liquid cream instantly into Chantilly.

TABLE OF CONTENTS

1

CREAMS & CO.

CREAMS

Vanilla custard 01
Confectioner's cream 02
Butter cream 03
Almond cream 04
Lemon curd 05
Chocolate mousse 06
Chocolate ganache 07
Panna cotta 08

SAUCES & TOPPINGS

Caramel 09
Salty butter caramel sauce 10
Chocolate sauce 11
Red berry coulis 12
Red berry compôte 13
Chantilly cream 14
Plain icing 15
Chocolate icing 16

2

SIMPLE CAKES

CLASSIC CAKES

Yogurt cake 17
Butter cake 18
Marbled cake 19

CHOCOLATE CAKES

Chocolate fondants 20
Flour-free chocolate cake 21
Brownies 22
Chocolate truffle cake 23

MADE IN THE U.S.A.

Carrot cake 24
Banana & walnut bread 25
Gingerbread 26
Corn bread 27

3

LAYERED CAKES

CHOUX PASTRY

Choux pastry 28
Praline choux 29
Caramel topping 30
Profiteroles 31
Chocolate éclairs 32
Choux puffs 33
Rose St-Honoré choux 34

PUFF PASTRY

Puff pastry 35
Mille-feuilles 36
Kings' cake 37

CHEESECAKES

Tiramisu 38
Mascarpone cheesecake 39
Corsican cheesecake 40

FILLED CAKES

Swiss roll 41
Coffee log 42
Poppyseed cake 43
Chocolate charlotte 44
Vacherin 45

4

LITTLE CAKES

French meringues 46
Blueberry muffins 47
Chocolate muffins 48
Banana muffins 49
Bran & raisin muffins 50
Oat & apple muffins 51
Madeleines 52
Chocolate macaroons 53
Raspberry macaroons 54
Caramel macaroons 55
Star buns 56
Doughnuts 57
Maple syrup glaze 58
Chocolate chip cookies 59
Almost Oreos® 60
Scones 61
Pecan biscuits 62
Breton biscuits 63
Blueberry pancakes 64
Eggy bread 65

5

TARTS

Sweet shortcrust pastry 66
Tarte tatin 67
Custard tart 68
Lemon meringue pie 69
Kiwi & mascarpone tartlets 70
Strawberry tartlets 71

INDEX OF RECIPES

Note: This index is organized by recipe number.

A

Almond cream 04
Almost Oreos® 60

B

Banana & walnut bread 25
Banana muffins 49
Blueberry muffins 47
Blueberry pancakes 64
Bran & raisin muffins 50
Breton biscuits 63
Brownies 22
Butter cake 18
Butter cream 03

C

Caramel 09
Caramel macaroons 55
Caramel topping 30
Carrot cake 24
Chantilly cream 14
Chocolate charlotte 44
Chocolate chip cookies 59
Chocolate éclairs 32
Chocolate fondants 20
Chocolate ganache 07
Chocolate icing 16
Chocolate macaroons 53
Chocolate mousse 06
Chocolate muffins 48
Chocolate sauce 11
Chocolate truffle cake 23
Choux pastry 28
Choux puffs 33
Coffee log 42
Confectioner's cream 02
Corn bread 27
Corsican cheesecake 40
Custard tart 68

D

Doughnuts 57

E

Eggy bread 65

F

Flour-free chocolate cake 21
French meringues 46

G

Gingerbread 26

K

Kings' cake 37
Kiwi & mascarpone tartlets 70

L

Lemon curd 05
Lemon meringue pie 69

M

Madeleines 52
Maple syrup glaze 58
Marbled cake 19
Mascarpone cheesecake 39
Mille-feuilles 36

O

Oat & apple muffins 51

P

Panna cotta 08

Pecan biscuits 62
Plain icing 15
Poppyseed cake 43
Praline choux 29
Profiteroles 31
Puff pastry 35

R

Raspberry macaroons 54
Red berry compôte 13
Red berry coulis 12
Rose St-Honoré choux 34

S

Salty butter caramel sauce 10
Scones 61
Star buns 56
Strawberry tartlets 71
Sweet shortcrust pastry 66
Swiss roll 41

T

Tarte tatin 67
Tiramisu 38

V

Vacherin 45
Vanilla custard 01

Y

Yogurt cake 17

GENERAL INDEX

Note: This index is organized by recipe number.

A

almonds
    Almond cream 04
    Chocolate macaroons 53
    Flour-free chocolate cake 21
    Kings' cake 37
    Poppyseed cake 43
    Strawberry tartlets 71
apples
    Oat & apple muffins 51
    Tarte tatin 67

B

bananas
    Banana & walnut bread 25
    Banana muffins 49
biscuits & cookies
    Almost Oreos® 60
    Breton biscuits 63
    Chocolate chip cookies 59
    Pecan biscuits 62
blueberries
    Blueberry muffins 47
    Blueberry pancakes 64
bread
    Banana & walnut bread 25
    Corn bread 27
    Gingerbread 26
butter
    Almond cream 04
    Breton biscuits 63
    Butter cake 18
    Butter cream 03
    Chocolate icing 16
    Coffee log 42
    Madeleines 52
    Salty butter caramel sauce 10

C

caramel
    Basic recipe 09
    Caramel macaroons 55
    Caramel topping 30
    Salty butter caramel sauce 10
cereals
    Bran & raisin muffins 50
    Oat & apple muffins 51
chantilly cream
    Basic recipe 14
    Mille-feuilles 36
    Rose St-Honoré choux 34
    Vacherin 45
cheesecakes
    Corsican cheesecake 40
    Mascarpone cheesecake 39
chocolate
    Almost Oreos® 60
    Brownies 22
    Chocolate charlotte 44
    Chocolate chip cookies 59
    Chocolate éclairs 32
    Chocolate fondants 20
    Chocolate ganache 07
    Chocolate icing 16
    Chocolate macaroons 53
    Chocolate mousse 06
    Chocolate muffins 48
    Chocolate sauce 11
    Chocolate truffle cake 23
    Flour-free chocolate cake 21
    Marbled cake 19
    Profiteroles 31
choux pastry
    Basic recipe 28
    Caramel topping 30
    Chocolate éclairs 32
    Choux puffs 33
    Praline choux 29
    Profiteroles 31

Rose St-Honoré choux 34
coffee
    Butter cream 03
    Coffee log 42
    Tiramisu 38
confectioner's cream
    Basic recipe 02
    Chocolate éclairs 32
    Kings' cake 37
    Mille-feuilles 36
    Rose St-Honoré choux 34
creams
    Almond cream 04
    Butter cream 03
    Chantilly cream 14
    Confectioner's cream 02
custard
    Custard tart 68
    Vanilla custard 01

D

dried fruit
    Bran & raisin muffins 50
    Carrot cake 24
    Scones 61

F

fruit
    Banana & walnut bread 25
    Banana muffins 49
    Blueberry muffins 47
    Blueberry pancakes 64
    Kiwi & mascarpone tartlets 70
    Lemon curd 05
    Lemon meringue pie 69
    Oat & apple muffins 51
    Raspberry macaroons 54
    Red berry compôte 13
    Red berry coulis 12

Strawberry tartlets 71
Tarte tatin 67
Vacherin 45

I

icing
Caramel topping 30
Carrot cake icing 24
Chocolate éclairs 32
Chocolate icing 16
Maple syrup glaze 58
Plain icing 15
Rose St-Honoré choux 34

L

lemon
Corsican cheesecake 40
Lemon curd 05
Lemon meringue pie 69
Yogurt cake 17

M

macaroons
Caramel macaroons 55
Chocolate macaroons 53
Raspberry macaroons 54
mascarpone
Kiwi & mascarpone
tartlets 70
Mascarpone cheesecake 39
Tiramisu 38
meringue
French meringues 46
Lemon meringue pie 69
Vacherin 45
mousse, chocolate
Basic recipe 06
Chocolate charlotte 44

muffins
Banana muffins 49
Blueberry muffins 47
Bran & raisin muffins 50
Chocolate muffins 48
Oat & apple muffins 51

N

nuts
Banana & walnut bread 25
Brownies 22
Carrot cake 24
Pecan biscuits 62

P

pastry
Choux pastry 28
Puff pastry 35
Sweet shortcrust pastry 66
puff pastry
Basic recipe 35
Kings' cake 37
Mille-feuilles 36

R

red berries
Red berry coulis 12
Red berry compôte 13

S

sauces
Chocolate sauce 11
Salty butter caramel sauce 10
Vanilla custard 01
shortcrust pastry
Basic recipe 66
Custard tart 68

Lemon meringue pie 69
Strawberry tartlets 71
Tarte tatin 67
spices
Carrot cake 24
Doughnuts 57
Gingerbread 26
strawberries
Eggy bread 65
Scones 61
Strawberry tartlets 71

T

tarts
Custard tart 68
Kiwi & mascarpone tartlets 70
Lemon meringue pie 69
Strawberry tartlets 71
Tarte tatin 67

V

vanilla
Banana & walnut bread 25
Butter cake 18
Butter cream 03
Chantilly cream 14
Chocolate chip cookies 59
Custard tart 68
Madeleines 52
Mascarpone cheesecake 39
Panna cotta 08
Star buns 56
Swiss roll 41
Vanilla custard 01

W

walnuts
Banana & walnut bread 25

ACKNOWLEDGEMENTS

My thanks to Emmanuel Le Vallois for his confidence in this project.

Also to Sonia and Fred Lucano for their superb work and for their encouragement when I needed it.

Thanks too to Rose-Marie Di Domenico for her tactful management of the work.

Thanks to Jérôme, for his help (lots of washing up!) and for tasting all the baking I presented him with at any hour of the day or night…

Finally, my thanks to Véronique Magnier for the books and recipes I inherited from her.

The author and publishers wish to thank Magimix for the loan of a mixer.
www.magimix.com

Props: Emmanuelle Javelle
Design: Alexandre Nicolas
English translation and adaptation: JMS Books llp
Layout: cbdesign